Stay in the Game

It's Too Soon To Quit

by

Van Crouch

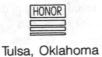

Tulsa, Oklahoma

Unless otherwise indicated, all Scripture quotations are taken from the *King James Version* of the Bible.

Stay in the Game
It's Too Soon To Quit
ISBN 0-89274-583-5
Copyright © 1989 by Van Crouch
1137 Wheaton Oaks Drive
Wheaton, Illinois 60187

Published by Honor Books
P. O. Box 55388
Tulsa, Oklahoma 74155

What Other People Say About Van Crouch...

"The coaches, players, and staff of the Chicago Bears truly appreciate your interest, leadership, and time spent in furthering and interpreting the 'Good News.' It is our wish that you will continue to help and inspire our players in the coming year. Thank you again for a job well done."

> Mike Ditka
> Head Football Coach
> Chicago Bears, NFL

"We are most fortunate to have acquired the services of a person such as yourself for the task ahead. You are playing an expanded role toward the continuation of our winning tradition. Thank you for your effort."

> Tom Landry
> Head Coach
> Dallas Cowboys

"Van, you have not only challenged and inspired us, but you have enabled us to more insightfully seek God's plan in both our personal and professional lives. We appreciate the new perspectives that you've given us through your ministry to us, and certainly we wholeheartedly appreciate you."

> James C. Dobson
> President,
> Focus on the Family
> Pomona, California

"Van Crouch relates Christian principles to contemporary problems with clarity and conviction. Splendid speaker!"

> Paul Harvey
> American Broadcasting Co.

"I'm just thankful that Van Crouch isn't an NFL linebacker, because he's the hardest-hitting speaker I've ever heard."

Walter Payton
Chicago Bears, NFL

"Here's hoping, Van, the day will come when we are able to do some work together. You do a marvelous job. God bless you and your activities."

Zig Ziglar

"Your talk to the Texaco Superstars group in Hawaii last week was one of the highlights of the trip. Your great sense of humor combined with your motivational comments had the audience alternately 'rolling in the aisles' and seriously contemplating your inspiring message."

J. W. Beard
Manager, Jobber Sales
Texaco, USA Marketing

"Our people were full of positive comments and upbeat reaction to the highly entertaining way you got your message across to us. You tailored the material nicely to follow the theme of our meeting."

John J. Puljung
General Manager
External Affairs
AT&T, Chicago

"Thank you so much for speaking at our chapel service before the Illinois game. Your message was very meaningful, and I appreciate the effort you made to attend."

Tom Osborne
Head Football Coach
University of Nebraska

DEDICATION

To Doni,
My crown and glory.
God's special gift to me.

CONTENTS

FOREWORD

Stay in the Game is a series of turning points. Every life is filled with turning points. Meeting my wife was a turning point, discovering the grace of God and his love for the world and his love through Jesus Christ was another turning point.

The birth of my children, teaching a Sunday school class, learning the joy of work, physical crises, financial crises were some of the many turning points in my life. Every turning point I can think of even though sometimes humiliating, costly or painful always brought me new dimensions of joy and thankfulness.

What comes to your mind when you think of the words "turning point"? It is possible you may feel many of your turning points were not for the better. I think that would be true in my life, too, except for two things: the people I've met and the books I've read.

I'll never be able to thank God enough for people I've met along life's way. Van Crouch is one of those people who has constantly reminded me that there are many who still want nothing more than God's way. I have observed him on the mountain tops and in the valleys and his joyful and thankful attitude have always said more than his words.

I'll never be able to thank God enough for the books he has put into my hands and sometimes just in the nick of time. I believe all my turning points could have been disasters had it not been for a book that helped add laughter to the tears and joy to the hurting heart.

Van Crouch is going to become a great friend to you as you discover much of his wisdom and experiences ring true in your own life. I'm glad I met Van, I'm glad I heard him speak and I'm tremendously glad he has taken time to share his ups and downs, his successes and failures, his joys and sorrows and his mind and heart. Van has packed his book with nourishment and ammunition to ensure your staying in the game.

The Apostle Paul is one of our great heroes. Here is his winning formula for staying in the game:

> *But none of these things move me, neither count I my life dear unto myself, so that I might finish my course with joy, and the ministry, which I have received of the Lord Jesus, to testify the gospel of the grace of God.*
>
> — Acts 20:24

— Charles "Tremendous" Jones

ACKNOWLEDGMENTS

Without people in our lives who reach out from time to time to give us a helping hand or a push onward toward our individual goals, none of us would ever fulfill our dreams and visions.

I have been blessed by knowing people who flavored my life and changed it; men who shared the good and the bad with me, who cared what happened to me, who laughed and cried with me; men who have positively affected my life. From the bottom of my heart, I want to thank these men, a "dynamic dozen," who have added depth and color to my days:

Sam Bender, midwest coordinator of Baseball Chapel, Inc., who opened the doors of major league baseball to me and ministered the love of God to me at the lowest point of my life; Dick Bestwick, athletic director of the University of South Carolina, who was tough on me because he really cared; Charles "T." Jones, whom God used to change my life; Doyle "Buddy" Harrison of Tulsa, Oklahoma, a master at encouragement without whose help this book would not have been possible; Pastor Van Gale of Wheaton, Illinois, who loved me through difficulties and convinced me I could make it; and Larry Kerychuk of Athletes International Ministry, whose prayer and diligence has resulted in the largest conference in America for professional athletes.

Also, John Kurowski of Denver, a sales and marketing genius, who demanded excellence and got it; Bob Nichols of Fort Worth, Texas, who encouraged me to keep going when I wanted to quit; Charles Nieman of El Paso, Texas, a man destined to win big in life; John Hummel, who knows how to build character; Randy St. Clair of Kansas City, Missouri, national vice-president of the Fellowship of Christian Athletes, whose influence has changed thousands of young lives; and Gerald Watson of Chicago, who is impossible to be around without becoming more enthusiastic, more excited, and more "turned on" to life itself.

Special Acknowledgment

I want to especially acknowledge Keith Provance of Tulsa. When it comes to doing the impossible, no one is better than Keith, vice president and general manager of Harrison House, Inc., and his dynamic staff. Harrison House operates with excellence and integrity.

It has been an exciting adventure working with this great firm, and it has been a joy and privilege to be associated with such a committed group of talented people.

INTRODUCTION:

My Promise to You

The reading, review, and digesting of these pages can be one of the most profitable things you have ever done.

How can I make such a promise?

For the past ten years, I have shared the concepts presented in this book to America's leading corporations, trade associations, and professional sports teams.

People from all walks of life have heard these concepts and ideas and have come to a turning point — a place where they made a quality decision to win rather than lose. The decision was theirs, and it will be yours.

Whether you are part of the corporate world, a super bowl or world series team member, or simply someone looking for some positive direction for your life — there is hope!

You have been given the power to choose to maintain your present level or go on to greatness. Nearly everyone has dreams for his life.

Do you have some dreams you would like to see become a reality?

Many times we fail to develop a plan or a blueprint and our dreams remain just dreams.

Someone has said, "Most people don't plan to fail, they simply fail to plan."

This book is a collection of some of the best ideas I have been exposed to from the successful corporate, sports, and ministry communities.

In the following pages are chapters dealing with key areas for a life that wins.

Read and study them carefully.

Learn them.

Apply them, and live by them.

Your success will be guaranteed.

There is a reason you picked up this book today. Possibly you have come to a place in life — as I did once — where you are tired of losing.

I have good news!

You are about to experience a turning point. Stay in the game — it's too soon to quit!

Van Crouch
Wheaton, Illinois

Stay in the Game

It's Too Soon To Quit

Chapter 1
IT'S TOO SOON TO QUIT

*The greatest revolution of our generation
is the discovery that human beings,
by changing the inner attitudes of their minds,
can change the outer aspects of their lives.*

— *William James*

☆☆☆☆☆☆☆☆☆☆☆☆☆☆☆☆☆☆☆☆☆☆☆☆

Why did you pick up this book today?

Are you tired, lacking in purpose, feeling life holds no excitement for you?

Maybe you are in one of life's many storms. A storm in your life may be a good sign. It can mean you have not yet been conquered! You are just meeting some opposition on the road to a miracle. So if you feel you have come to the end of your rope, tie a knot and hang on. Read on.

☆☆☆☆☆☆☆☆☆☆☆☆☆☆☆☆☆☆☆☆☆☆☆

There is hope for you.

☆☆☆☆☆☆☆☆☆☆☆☆☆☆☆☆☆☆☆☆☆☆☆

This is not another self-help book. It is not a "positive mental attitude" book that suggests a new way of thinking will cause life's problems to disappear and make you an overnight success. However, I do hope you will see that:

> *It makes little difference*
> *what's happening out there.*
> *It's how you take it*
> *and what you make of it that counts.* [1]
> — Denis Waitley

Take a look at the current best seller list.

Many self-improvement and business books focus on success. They often give beautiful examples which you and I cannot utilize. You may be impressed or even awed by some corporate superstar's outstanding achievement — but you end up frustrated.

It is not always uplifting to read about the excellence of others when your own life seems to resemble that of Job.

All too often many of these positive-thinking formulas become negative, because the result of reading them is that you wind up feeling deficient.

Unfortunately, many "how-to, self-help" books do not deal with the reality of failure; but it happens and is sometimes very painful.

My Personal Storm

If you had met me a few years ago, you would have seen a depressed, despondent, and discouraged man — and those were my strong points! No area of my life was going well. I was failing in business, personal finances, and most importantly, in my family.

In 1968, I left Colorado State University where I had been coaching football and moved to Chicago. American Express hired me to represent them in their Money Order Division. They gave me a sales territory on the tough "crime-ridden" south side of the city.

The area I worked in was so tough that the police had an unlisted phone number!

When the gangster, Al Capone, lived there he worked as an Avon lady!

However, in my quest for achievement and recognition, I soon managed to set records and move up the management ladder.

After working for American Express, I went into the insurance business as an agent for the New York Life Insurance Company. They gave me a rate book and a mirror. The rate book was to calculate how much the policies cost, and the mirror was to watch myself starve to death. It was tough!

In those early days, I sold furniture to supplement my income. I sold my couch, my stereo, and my television! But after a very difficult start-up period, business began to turn around.

By July 1975, I was a consistent qualifier for the prestigious Million Dollar Round Table and in the top 6 percent of New York Life's more than 9,000 agents. Business was good, the cash was flowing. I was busy collecting plaques and trophies, trying hard to keep up with the Joneses. I just didn't realize the Joneses weren't going anywhere!

At one point my Master Charge card was stolen. I did not report it missing for six months because the guy that took it was spending less than my wife! And that brings me to the next area where I was failing.

Family Time, a publication of the insurance industry's Million Dollar Round Table, has said "No success in business substitutes for failure in the home."[2]

My success track record came to a screeching halt as divorce loomed on the scene during the spring of 1979. It was a crisis from which I thought I would never recover. There were many days when my biggest effort was to get out of bed. Depression took its toll. Life for me was out of control.

The healing process was slow. But little by little, my mind was renewed, and the desire to go on with life came back.

In the meantime, fearing rejection, insurance sales became difficult. I was like the little boy who came home from school with his report card, and his father inquired, "Why are your grades so poor?"

The boy answered, "Father, don't feel so badly. I got the highest mark of anybody that failed."

My report was not good and I was hurting in every area of life.

It was quite a rocky road — up one day and down the next. However, in the midst of chaos, I began to experience some life-changing principles, such as these:

- "Achievers know that life is a self-fulfilling prophecy.

- "The amazing truth is that every individual tends to receive what he or she expects in the long run."[3]

"God Did Not Put Us on This Earth So That We Might Fail."[4]

A close personal friend and great speaker, Charles "Tremendous" Jones, says:

"Any time you choose to move to a higher dimension of living, there's always going to come a time when you want to quit. It's a natural feeling. But there's a difference between wanting to quit and having to quit. You can enjoy the feeling of wanting to quit because you know you are not going to quit."[5]

You may ask, "How do you know this is true, Crouch?"

I know because you are reading this book.

> There *is* hope!
> Stay in the game!
> Play one more set of downs,
>   another inning,
>   run another mile.
> You *can* make it.

One day it dawned on my lightning-quick mind that being a benchwarmer in life is a matter of choice. Most people are grossly under-utilized. Achievers are made — not born! We have the choice to be the exception and win big. The greatest force on earth is a human soul set on fire.

Life Is Not a Spectator Sport

All too often life is approached as a spectator sport, i.e., football. There are eighty thousand people in the stands desperately needing exercise, while there are twenty-two on the field badly in need of rest!

The fact is that success in life or any worthwhile endeavor is conditional. There are some prerequisites.

Webster defines prerequisite as:

"Something that is necessary to an end or to the carrying out of a function."[6]

Regardless of the problems, there are some conditions that must be met to experience victory. Now that you have invested your time and money in this book — make a decision to win!

☆☆☆☆☆☆☆☆☆☆☆☆☆☆☆☆☆☆☆☆☆☆☆☆

"One man with courage makes a majority."
— Andrew Jackson

☆☆☆☆☆☆☆☆☆☆☆☆☆☆☆☆☆☆☆☆☆☆☆☆

Not long ago I had the privilege of having lunch in Chicago with Notre Dame football coach, Lou Holtz.

Holtz said that, to him, the word *win* means: "*W*hat's *I*mportant *N*ow."

It is important to let the past be past at last. You cannot unscramble eggs! It is useless to look back — unless that is the direction you plan to go. What lies behind or ahead is not nearly as important as what lies within.

From within, decide to win!

Success in life begins with your decision to succeed. The One who created you and me does not have the words *lose, hopeless, no way out, incurable* or *beyond repair* in His vocabulary. As human beings, we have been given a will. We have the right to make decisions.

Whose decision is it to achieve? Yours.

Whose decision is it to fail? Yours.

Wholeness, fulfillment, purpose, and success hinge on your decision.

Steven Brown, president of the Fortune Group, says, "Essentially there are two actions in life: Performance and excuses. Make a decision as to which you will accept from yourself."[7]

Brown goes on to say, "We may predict and calculate the amount of failure an individual will experience by this formula: People fail in direct proportion to their willingness to accept socially acceptable excuses for failure."[8]

It is time to take responsibility for your choices and actions.

The Purpose of This Book:
To Help You Reach a Turning Point

As Zig Ziglar says, "You do not 'pay the price' for success, you 'enjoy the price.' "[9]

Decide to move ahead while others ask for answers.

Look beyond the risks,
obstacles,
and hardships.

☆ ☆

You can live a life that counts.

☆ ☆

The late Vince Lombardi put some of his philosophy concerning winning on paper entitled, "The Habit of Winning."

Says Lombardi:

"Winning is not a sometime thing. You don't win once-in-awhile. You don't do things right once-in-awhile. You do them right all the time. Winning is a habit. Unfortunately, so is losing.

"It is a reality of life that men are competitive and the most competitive games draw the most competitive men. That's why they're there — to compete. They know the rules and the objectives when they get in the game. The objective is to win — fairly, squarely, decently, by the rules — but to win. And in truth, I have never known a man worth his salt who in the long run, deep down in his heart, did not appreciate the grind — the discipline. There is something in good men that really yearns for...needs...discipline and the harsh reality of head-to-head combat.

"I don't say these things because I believe in the 'brute' nature of man, or that men must be brutalized to be combative. I believe in God and I believe in human decency. But I firmly believe that any man's finest hour, his greatest fulfillment to all he holds dear, is the moment when he has worked his heart out in a good cause and lies exhausted on the field of battle victorious."

It's true!

You *can* be the person you want to be.

✩ ✩

Have what you want out of life.

✩ ✩

Dr. Heartsill Wilson of Denver, Colorado, said it this way:

"This is the beginning of a new day.

"God has given me this day to use as I will. I can waste it — or use it for good, but what I do today is important, because I am exchanging a day of my life for it!

"When tomorrow comes, this day will be gone forever, leaving in its place something that I have traded for it.

"I want it to be gain,
    and not loss;
good, and not evil;
    success, and not failure;
in order that I shall not regret
    the price that I have paid for it."

If you can relate to any of my story, then I have good news: Failure is not final!

It is always too soon to quit.

Endnotes

[1]Waitley, Denis. *The Joy of Working* (New York: Dodd, Mead & Company. Copyright © 1985 by Larimi Communications Associates, Inc.).

[2]Ibid. p. xi.

[3]Ibid. p. 72, 73.

[4]Ibid. p. 73.

[5]Jones, Charles T. "The Price of Leadership," (Cassette), Harrisburg, Pennsylvania.

[6]Webster's *Dictionary*.

[7]Brown, Steven W. *13 Fatal Errors Managers Make and How You Can Avoid Them* (Berkley 1987), p. 3.

[8]Ibid.

[9]Ziglar, Zig. *See You at the Top* (Dallas: Pelican Publishing Company. Copyright © 1975 by Zig Ziglar), p. 185. Used by permission of the Pelican Publishing Co.

Chapter 2
Caution: Construction Work Ahead

Where there is no vision, the people perish.
— Proverbs 29:18

☆☆☆☆☆☆☆☆☆☆☆☆☆☆☆☆☆☆☆☆☆☆☆☆

The two basics for personal success are:

1) A *vision* — "a mental sight, dream, or revelation."

2) *A commitment to the vision.*

Exactly what is a vision?

A vision, or a goal, provides specific direction. Without a vision, you *have* no direction. To achieve, you must have an idea of what you want to achieve.

✩ ✩

If you don't know where you are going,
you will probably wind up somewhere else. [1]
— David Campbell

✩ ✩

When I grew up, our home was not run like "Leave It to Beaver" or "Father Knows Best." How thankful I am today for a Christian mother who knew how to stay in the game on her knees before the Lord, praying for me. It made a tremendous difference not only in life but in my brother's life as well.

One of the earliest examples of a vision and goal was when I got involved in high school football in my hometown of Grove City, Pennsylvania. A man named Dick Bestwick came to coach football. He became a legend. Presently he is athletic director at the University of South Carolina.

His practices were endurance contests. They were hard, hot, dirty and tough. Playing a game was almost like taking a night off. He built a tremendous winning record. More important, Bestwick and his staff worked to build character. He taught what it is to win, to be honest, to give our best. Class attendance was not optional, and respect for parents was a must.

At times, we referred to Coach Bestwick's office as a pool table. If it was necessary for him to call you in, he was likely to grab you by the shirt and bounce you off all four walls. As an educator and coach, he cared enough to confront.

As young men, we learned if we would choose to be tough on ourselves, life would be easier on us. It has always made a positive difference in my life when I have someone to be accountable to. Sound leadership will cause you to develop a vision and rise to a higher level.

Many people today, including Christians, have no vision. They do not know where they are going in life.

As I often say when I speak, the mortality rate in America is running one out of one. Everyone will die sometime.

I used to tell my prospects, "John, when they back the hearse up to the front door, they are not making a practice run!"

Therefore, it is important to make a quality decision to make the best of your life — to be the best you can, not only for Jesus, if you are a Christian, but for personal fulfillment.

☆ ☆

"Cheshire-Puss, . . . would you tell me, please, which way I ought to go from here?"

"That depends a good deal on where you want to get to," said the Cat.

"I don't care much where —" said Alice.

"Then it doesn't matter which way you go," said the Cat.

"— so long as I get somewhere," Alice added as an explanation.

"Oh, you're sure to do that," said the Cat, "if you only walk long enough."[2]

— Lewis Carroll

☆☆☆☆☆☆☆☆☆☆☆☆☆☆☆☆☆☆☆☆☆☆☆☆

Many of us run our lives as Alice did her trip through "Wonderland." If we "do not care much where" we end up, we just keep wandering around.

People with no purpose in life never get anywhere. He who expects little will not be disappointed!

☆☆☆☆☆☆☆☆☆☆☆☆☆☆☆☆☆☆☆☆☆☆☆☆

Destiny is not a matter of chance;
it is a matter of choice.

☆☆☆☆☆☆☆☆☆☆☆☆☆☆☆☆☆☆☆☆☆☆☆☆

A goal gives you a specific direction to work toward.

Specific direction will keep you from wasting effort and time.

If your goal is to get from one city to another, you do not go off in some other direction and wander around, but proceed on course as quickly as possible. Wandering around makes you unstable, or double-minded. Then you will be like the waves of the sea, tossed to and fro, and will not receive anything when you pray. (James 1:7,8.)

☆ ☆

Knowing your destination is half the journey.[3]

☆ ☆

In *See You at the Top*, Zig Ziglar says:

"Do most people have goals? Apparently not. You can stop a hundred young men on any street and ask each one, 'What are you doing that will absolutely guarantee your failure in life?'

"After recovering from their initial shock, each one will probably say, 'What do you mean, what am I doing to guarantee my failure? I'm working for success.'

"Tragically, most of them think they are, but...if we follow those hundred young men until they are sixty-five years old, only five of them will have achieved financial security. Only one will be wealthy. You can get better odds than that in Las Vegas. ...Do the people in life who don't succeed actually plan to fail? I don't think so. The problem is they don't plan *anything*."[4]

☆ ☆

Happiness, wealth, and success are by-products of goal setting; they cannot be the goal themselves.[5]

☆ ☆

Three Reasons Why Visions and Goals Are Necessary

1. They provide purpose and motivation.

2. They provide specific direction.

3. They keep you single-minded on accomplishment.

In the area of purpose and motivation, having a goal and vision to work toward, to attain, will keep you motivated. If people lose motivation and purpose, they usually die fairly quickly afterwards. Also, many times, people *die* on the inside before their bodies die. They rust out before they wear out.

When I came home from work one night, my son asked, "Dad, what have you been doing all day?"

I said, "Nothing much."

He said, "Well, how did you know when you were finished?"

My son was right! Without specific direction, you do not know which way to go nor when you have arrived. Having a vision and a goal will give you that direction.

☆ ☆

The poorest man is not he who is without a cent,
but he who is without a dream. [6]
— Pennsylvania School Journal

☆ ☆

When asked how he climbed Mt. Everest, suppose Sir Edmund Hillary replied:

"I don't know. The missus and I just went out for a walk one afternoon, and before we knew it, there we were at the top."

Of course, that is *not* how Sir Edmund Hillary became the first man to reach the top of Mt. Everest. He had a vision: to be the first man to achieve this climb. And he had a goal: to reach the top of the mountain that had been called impossible to climb.

To achieve his vision and goal required planning, getting together supplies and equipment, finding a guide, and putting together a team. More importantly, however, it took sticking to the job at hand, persevering toward his vision and goal. Ziglar also wrote:

"Do you have a target or a goal? You must have a goal because it's just as difficult to reach a destination you don't have as it is to come back from a place where you've never been."[7]

The Apostle Paul said in Philippians 3:14 that he was pressing on toward the mark of the high calling.

He was saying, "I keep going for the goal to fulfill the vision. I keep the goal in front of me."

A goal and vision will keep you single-minded. For example, if you need money, you should set a specific amount as a goal and a specific date by which to reach that goal. A goal cannot be set for some nebulous time in the future. It must be specific and direct, and there needs to be a deadline.

Single-mindedness is a sign of excellence because it is the single-minded person who wins. He works in a specific direction to accomplish his goal. People with a poor sense of direction in life often get lazy.

Not having a goal results in no direction, but too *many* goals result in a lack of single-mindedness. Being overextended means being tired all the time.

☆ ☆

One of the essentials of a good swimming stroke is that it provides a rest period. No matter how efficient may be the pull with the arms, or the kick with the legs, unless there is a regular time, however brief it may be, when the arms and legs can rest, the swimmer soon becomes exhausted. With his threefold nature — spiritual, mental, and physical — man needs to pause or rest, if he would maintain efficiency. [8]

☆ ☆

Inspirational Dissatisfaction

Fortunately, I was blessed with a quality I call *inspirational dissatisfaction*. Not being satisfied with where I was, I could believe in my heart there was something bigger and better and move on from there.

Charles Jones in his best-selling book, *Life Is Tremendous,* said:

"The real work is not hard work or difficult work or the actual functions that we perform, the real work is to get excited about your work and that takes work."[9]

In order to become excited about your work, you must be excited about your goal.

The greatest limitations in life are self-imposed. So go for it!

☆☆☆☆☆☆☆☆☆☆☆☆☆☆☆☆☆☆☆☆☆☆☆

"There's no such thing as coulda, shoulda and woulda. If you shoulda and coulda, you woulda done it."
Pat Riley
Los Angeles Lakers coach

☆☆☆☆☆☆☆☆☆☆☆☆☆☆☆☆☆☆☆☆☆☆☆

A *vision* is a pictured goal.

☆☆☆☆☆☆☆☆☆☆☆☆☆☆☆☆☆☆☆☆☆☆☆

Endnotes

[1]Campbell, Dr. David. *If You Don't Know Where You're Going, You Will Probably Wind Up Somewhere Else* (Argus Communications, 1974).

[2]Carroll, Lewis. *Alice in Wonderland* (New York: Washington Square Press, Inc., 1951, 1960), p. 56.

[3]Waitley. *Joy*, p. 43.

[4]Ziglar. *See You*, p. 149.

[5]Waitley. *Joy*, p. 39.

[6]Tan, Paul Lee. *Encyclopedia of 7700 Illustrations* (Maryland: Rockville, Assurance Publishers. Copyright © 1979 by Paul Lee Tan, ninth printing), p. 1566, Epigram.

[7]Ziglar. *See You*, p. 148.

[8]Tan. *Encyclopedia*, p. 114, #5007.

[9]Jones, Charles. *Life Is Tremendous* (Wheaton: Tyndale House Publishers. Copyright © 1981).

Chapter 3
BY THE INCH,
IT'S A CINCH!

All big men are dreamers.
They see things in the soft haze of a spring day
or in the red fire
of a long winter's evening.

Some of us let these great dreams die, but others nourish
and protect them, nurse them through bad days till they bring
them to the sunshine and light which come always to those
who sincerely hope that their dreams will come true. [1]

— Woodrow Wilson

☆☆☆☆☆☆☆☆☆☆☆☆☆☆☆☆☆☆☆☆☆☆☆☆

The name *Solomon* has become synonymous with
wisdom.

My friend, author-teacher Mike Murdock has found
seventeen "secrets" or principles in the story of King

Solomon's successful building of the great temple in Jerusalem.[2]

These principles will work for you and for me, not just for kings and rulers.

1. He established a clear-cut goal. (2 Chron. 2:1.)

2. He received God's stamp of approval for his project. (2 Chron. 7:16.)

3. He announced the goal and explained its value and purpose. (2 Chron. 2:3,4.)

4. He valued the greatness of His goal and was proud of it. (2 Chron. 2:5.)

5. He developed a detailed plan. (2 Chron. 3:3-5.)

6. He acknowledged his limitations. (2 Chron. 2:6.)

7. He established a reputation of integrity. (2 Chron. 2:12.)

8. He consulted other achievers related to his project. (2 Chron. 2:3.)

9. He acknowledged past favors and asked for assistance. (2 Chron. 2:3.)

10. He set a first-class level of quality. (2 Chron. 3:6,7.)

11. He involved as many people as possible in the project. (2 Chron. 2:17,18.)

12. He organized and delegated responsibilities. (2 Chron. 2:18.)

13. He used the expertise of specialists. (2 Chron. 2:7,14.)

14. He made the description and details of all contracts clear. (2 Chron. 2:10,11,15.)

15. He compensated and rewarded those who assisted him in achieving his goal. (2 Chron. 2:10.)

16. He kept alive the enthusiasm and greatness of his project. (2 Chron. 2:9.)

17. He established a production schedule and began the work. (2 Chron. 2:3;5:1.)

☆ ☆

Recipe for Success

1. Take a dream.

2. Mix it with motivation + action.

3. Add long hours of practice + discipline.

Yield: *Your goal, whatever it may be.*[3]

☆ ☆

Goals may be broken down as follows: *long-range goals, medium-range goals, short-range goals, minigoals,* and *microgoals.*

Long-range goals are concerned with the overall style of life, for example, the type of job you want, to be married or not, the kind of family you want, and the general situation in which you wish to live.

Although you develop some overall idea of what you are after, do not make long-range plans in too much detail because change *will* come along. It is more important to have an overall, flexible plan.

When I think of a flexible plan, I think of a statement I heard Charles Jones make:

> "A flexible plan says that whatever can go wrong will go wrong, and you had better plan on it going wrong, so when it goes wrong, that's your plan. If something goes right, you can work it in."

Medium-range goals are those covering the next five years or so. They can cover a particular training or education you are seeking or the next step in your career. These goals become somewhat more exciting because you have more control over them and can tell along the way whether you are going to achieve them. Then you can increase or modify your efforts accordingly.

☆☆☆☆☆☆☆☆☆☆☆☆☆☆☆☆☆☆☆☆☆☆☆

Knowing your destination is half the journey.[4]

☆☆☆☆☆☆☆☆☆☆☆☆☆☆☆☆☆☆☆☆☆☆☆

Short-range goals are those covering the period from about one month to one year. You can set these goals quite realistically and tell fairly soon whether you are reaching them. Do not set impossible goals. You want to stretch yourself, but you do not want to get discouraged. Aim realistically, then try hard to achieve your aims.

Minigoals are those covering about one month. You have much more control over these. You can plan a reasonable program for the next week or the next month, and your chances of carrying them out are good. If you find you have planned too ambitiously, you can modify for a period after that. By thinking in shorter periods of time, you have more control over each.

Microgoals cover the next fifteen minutes to one hour. Realistically, these are the only goals you have direct control over. Because of this, although microgoals are modest in impact, they are extraordinarily important in your life. For it is only through these microgoals that you can attain the larger goals.

☆☆☆☆☆☆☆☆☆☆☆☆☆☆☆☆☆☆☆☆☆☆

A journey of a thousand miles begins with a single step.

☆☆☆☆☆☆☆☆☆☆☆☆☆☆☆☆☆☆☆☆☆☆

If you do not make any progress toward your long-range goals in the next fifteen minutes, when will you?

The following fifteen minutes, or the fifteen after that?

Sooner or later, you are going to have to pick fifteen minutes and get going.

You should plan your microgoals well and then make progress toward that goal:

"I'm going to start that term paper right now."

"I'm going to learn that new sales technique now."

"I'm going to make that next call right now."

Then your long-range goals will take care of themselves. However, do remember to keep them flexible, in order to allow for changes in your personal life, your career, or the world in general.

☆☆☆☆☆☆☆☆☆☆☆☆☆☆☆☆☆☆☆☆☆☆☆☆☆

Whether you believe you can do a thing
or believe you can't, you are right.
— Henry Ford

☆☆☆☆☆☆☆☆☆☆☆☆☆☆☆☆☆☆☆☆☆☆☆☆☆

In general, the longer range the goal the less control you have over achieving it. If, for example, one of your long-range goals is to become a famous pianist or racquetball player, there is little you can do about it today. You cannot go out and brew up an instant success.

In contrast you have a lot more control over microgoals.

If you play raquetball, you can say to yourself, "In the next hour I'm going to master the kill shot. I'm going to go into the court and hit 250 shots by myself, working on technique."

And you can do it. One shot will not make you famous, but it is a necessary step towards winning a racquetball tournament, or achieving your goal. The point is the only kind of planning you have direct control over are the modest little goals.

The trick of planning a successful life is to stack together these smaller goals in a way that increases your chances of reaching the long-range goals you really care about.

In at least one area of your life, be intense. Focus strongly on something, whether it is your job, a hobby, or some group activity.

Be good at something — good enough so that you can take pride in knowing that you are a valuable person.

Knowing you can do at least one thing well builds self-esteem.

Plan for Intensity

To do this requires dedication, determination, and persistance. However, it is almost impossible to be dedicated, determined, and persistent in all areas, so do not try. Pick one area and excel in it.

If you pick the right area, then a lot of other things will fall in line. You will find this draws people to you, builds self-esteem, gives you a sense of achievement, and causes you to feel good about yourself.

Plan some diversity in your life, even when you are focusing on one area. Life is full of changes. The best protection against trauma when major change occurs is diversity in your talents, in your assets. In planning, pay attention to this fact. Consider some other things that you may be able to do with excellence.

In developing your vision, plan for gradual improvement, not spectacular leaps.

☆☆☆☆☆☆☆☆☆☆☆☆☆☆☆☆☆☆☆☆☆☆☆☆

Write the vision, and make it plain upon tables,
that he may run that readeth it.
For the vision is yet for an appointed time,
but at the end it shall speak, and not lie:
though it tarry, wait for it;
because it will surely come,
it will not tarry.

— Habakkuk 2:2,3

☆☆☆☆☆☆☆☆☆☆☆☆☆☆☆☆☆☆☆☆☆☆☆☆

God told the children of Israel, "I'll drive them (heathen in the Promised Land) out of the land before you, little by little. Otherwise, you would be too few to keep the wild beasts and the untamed plants, vines, and weeds from overrunning the country." (Deut. 7:22; author's paraphrase.)

Practically everything worthwhile in life is achieved in small steps:

Education is gained gradually.

Babies grow up one day at a time.

A beautiful garden is designed and grows slowly.

Talents are developed over time.

Athletic ability increases with practice.

Relationships are forged, and deep affection develops gradually.

Each of our lives is a series of gradual campaigns in a number of different areas: the job, family, and friends.

Nature provides many guidelines here. A slow and steady stream of water will in time erode the hardest rock. A small insignificant sprout, in time, will slowly and almost imperceptibly turn into a mighty oak. Almost unnoticed, a child in time will grow to an independent adult. Recognize the gradual progressions of life and the power of time.

☆☆☆☆☆☆☆☆☆☆☆☆☆☆☆☆☆☆☆☆☆☆☆☆☆

Planning is the bridge
linking dreams and achievement. [5]

☆☆☆☆☆☆☆☆☆☆☆☆☆☆☆☆☆☆☆☆☆☆☆☆☆

A few final thoughts on planning:

To plan you must have information. You must know something about the area in which you are working, something about the subject of your plans.

• If you are trying to plan something about your education, you must know the educational options available to you.

• If you are trying to plan your career or future, you must know about jobs.

• If you are trying to plan your future home, you must know about housing and real estate.

To accumulate this knowledge, you have to do some digging:

• You have to read books, pamphlets, magazines, anything relevant that you can get your hands on.

• You have to talk to knowledgeable people, a wide range of them.

• You have to accumulate some experiences for yourself. Virtually anything that educates you is worthwhile, so seek out some experiences in the area you are planning.

The point is you cannot plan until you have some raw material to plan with. You need knowledge and experience.

A Price To Pay

Also, there is a price to pay to achieve goals.

There is a price to pay for anything you decide to go after.

If you do not take time to count the cost, or the price, that you are going to pay to achieve your goals, you could end up with "egg on your face," looking like a fool. You could come up desperately short.

One thing to ask yourself when considering goals and objectives is, "How far am I willing to push myself to produce?"

Jesus taught in the Beatitudes, "Blessed are they which do hunger and thirst after righteousness: for they shall be filled." (Matt. 5:6.)

To achieve your vision and goal, you need to make a whole-hearted commitment.

How does commitment pertain to achieving goals?

Webster defined commitment as "to put into total trust."[6]

Commitment is a quality decision which you, and you alone, can make to accept full responsibility to carry your vision to completion no matter what the cost.

Someone has said, "Commit your vision to God, and yourself to the vision."

It is a decision, an act of your will to "sell out to the cause."

Some say that blessings are always on the other side of commitment.

There are a number of working purposes and benefits of commitment:

• Commitment releases the wisdom and power of God into a situation.

• Commitment also releases depth and detail of the vision.

• Commitment will enable you to maintain a right mental attitude, to stay on course, because once you make a commitment, you will find a lot of opportunities to quit.

• Commitment to the vision will activate the force of patience.

When vision is combined with commitment, it becomes a powerful force. With the vision is hope. Hope is a confident expectation, which is future tense. The goal you desire to achieve gives you a direct target to hit, a blueprint to give substance to, a plan to release faith into in order to bring a desired result to pass.

☆☆☆☆☆☆☆☆☆☆☆☆☆☆☆☆☆☆☆☆☆☆☆☆

"By the inch it's a cinch, but by the yard, it's hard to stay at it until it comes to pass."

☆☆☆☆☆☆☆☆☆☆☆☆☆☆☆☆☆☆☆☆☆☆☆☆

Making a commitment will help you keep the vision, and the key is "priorities."

You will not be able to do everything for everyone, but because of your vision and your commitment to the vision, priorities will come into focus. The vision becomes your focal point.

If you are focusing on the vision, you are not focusing on the problems. The vision will become bigger than the problems. The problems then become steps to achieve the vision.

Frank Sullivan C.L.U. in his excellent book, *The Critical Path to Sales Success,*[7] lists a four-point formula to success:

1. *Decide what you want to make of yourself.*

He says, "Write it all out." Make a commitment. Give yourself a reason to get out of bed.

☆ ☆

The will to win is worth nothing
unless you have the will to prepare.

☆ ☆

At seminar presentations, I tell people the first thing on my "to-do" list is: "Get up!"

The reason that is important is because usually people do not die upright, they die in bed!

I get up when the first ray of dawn hits my window. (Fortunately, my window faces the west.)

2. *Decide how you are going to do it.*

A vision minus a plan is simply a dream. Be sure and write it all out.

Someone has said, "Onto paper, off your mind."

3. *Develop a written checklist on yourself.*

This is because the people who break records keep records.

4. Perhaps the most important suggestion of Sullivan is: *Do it.*

Get started getting started. Start today.

I add a fifth suggestion:

Set an acceptable bottomline, or base. Write down what is the least you are going to do.

Dr. Kenneth Blanchard in his *One Minute Manager* says people do better when they feel better about themselves.[8] One way to feel better about yourself is to set a goal you can reach, a "do-able" goal. Then when you reach that one, you will begin to believe you can make it, and set a little harder goal the next time.

Another idea from Mike Murdock is: "One goal all people have in common is to be happy."[9]

Happiness is feeling good about yourself.

Achievements generate internal contentment. Most people have a need to feel as if they are achieving something in life.

Achievements generate energy, aliveness, vitality, and a sense of worth, but there can be no achievement unless you first set clear-cut goals.

Winners Are Achievers

Winners are people who have a vision — who know how to set goals for themselves. In his Study Guide, "Five Keys for Achieving Goals," Mike Murdock lists some points that I have adapted for this book. I believe they will help you in achieving your goals:[10]

1. *Be aware of the purpose of goal-setting.* For the winner a goal is not an idea, a wish, a thought, or fantasy, it is an objective he sincerely intends to accomplish.

2. *Set goals to avoid energy waste* of non-essentials, to concentrate mental abilities, time and energy on projects that are fulfilling and worthwhile.

3. *Set goals to maintain interest* which stimulates you to action and alerts your mind.

4. *Set goals for a sense of progress.*

However, you need to recognize four obstacles to overcome in goal-setting.

1. *Lack of understanding* its importance because of prejudiced teaching, or lack of teaching.

Some might say, "I don't want to put myself in a box...I want to stop and smell the roses...Whatever will be will be."

2. *Fear of failure.*

Setting goals creates a responsibility to yourself and others to succeed. Rebelling against possible penalties and rejections if you do not succeed.

3. *Unreasonable goals.* You might be living up to the expectations of others. You may have misjudged your abilities, the timing or number of goals you can handle.

4. *Lack of training,* or being told to do it, but never taught *how* to do it. Frustrated, you simply fail to have a vision and fail to set goals and objectives.

☆ ☆

Quality is never an accident;
it is always the result of high intention,
sincere effort, intelligent direction,
and skillful execution;
it represents the wise choice
of many alternatives.

— Willa A. Foster

☆ ☆

Endnotes

[1]Waitley. *Joy,* p. 31, 32.

[2]Murdock, Mike. "Solomon's Seventeen Secrets for Achievement," Mike Murdock Evangelistic Association, Dallas, Texas.

[3]Waitley. *Joy,* p. 38.

[4]Ibid., p. 43.

[5]Ibid., p. 46.

[6]Webster's Dictionary.

[7]Sullivan, Frank. *The Critical Path to Sales Success.* Copyright held by The Research and Review Service of America, Inc., 1720 E. 38th St., Indianapolis, Indiana 46218.

[8]Blanchard, Dr. Kenneth and Johnson, Spencer. *One Minute Manager* (New York: William Morrow and Co., Inc. Copyright © 1982.)

[9]Murdock.

[10]Murdock. "Five Keys for Achieving Goals." A Mike Murdock Study Guide.

Chapter 4

ATTITUDE: THE DIFFERENCE BETWEEN LIVING AND EXISTING

Famed economist Stuart Chase once sat down to figure the calendar of his days. There is, he said, an ascending scale of human values and somewhere on it there is a line between living and mere existing. In how many hours of the week, he asked himself, had he truly and intensively lived? In how many had he just existed? Out of the 168 hours of the week, he found that he had been "alive" only 40, or about 25 percent of the time. [1]

— *Woman's Day*

☆ ☆

If you would like to have greater earnings in the next year, enjoy life more, reduce fatigue and procrastination, increase effectiveness, get along better with your peers, contribute more to society, improve family relationships and possibly improve your health — then a right mental attitude is critical.

One thing that everyone seems to agree on is that the attitude with which you undertake a project is a dominant factor in whether it is accomplished successfully or not.

✩✩✩✩✩✩✩✩✩✩✩✩✩✩✩✩✩✩✩✩✩✩✩✩

*Attitude more than aptitude will
determine your altitude.*

✩✩✩✩✩✩✩✩✩✩✩✩✩✩✩✩✩✩✩✩✩✩✩✩

William James, the father of American psychology, said the most important discovery of our time is that we can alter our lives by altering our attitudes.[2]

The good news is that if we do not like the attitude we have, it can be changed.

✩✩✩✩✩✩✩✩✩✩✩✩✩✩✩✩✩✩✩✩✩✩✩✩

*A pessimist is one sitting on the premises
rather than standing on the promises.
An optimist is a person who takes action,
who moves out ahead of the crowd.*

✩✩✩✩✩✩✩✩✩✩✩✩✩✩✩✩✩✩✩✩✩✩✩✩

Someone paused to ask a man on the street if it was National Apathy Week, and he replied, "I don't know, and I don't care!"

Attitudes Are Contagious

Over the past ten years I have worked with the Chicago Bears football team in a voluntary capacity. In 1982, there was a transition which brought Mike Ditka, formerly a Hall of Fame tight end for the Bears and later a coach for the Dallas Cowboys, back to the Bears as coach.

One of the first things Ditka attempted to instill in the Bears was that they all played for the same organization. That may sound odd, but at the time Ditka came, the offense did not like the defense, and the defense did not like the offense. There was a competitiveness within the team that would better have been turned on an opposing team during a game.

Sometimes the hitting was more intense at practice than during an actual game.

Doug Plank, the Bears' great defensive safety who had played at Ohio State University, was quoted as saying: "Since Coach Ditka came to the Bears, we have more unity. This year, I have decided to learn the names of some of the offensive players!"

Ditka worked, firstly, to have unity, to get everyone going in the same direction; then secondly, and possibly most important, he worked on attitude in order to convince the team they could win.

Three years later, the Bears were the 1985 Super Bowl champions.

What turned the team around? Yes, they had great talent on the team, but I believe the key factor was a positive mental attitude. A positive attitude will have positive results, because:

☆☆☆☆☆☆☆☆☆☆☆☆☆☆☆☆☆☆☆☆☆☆☆

Attitudes are contagious.

☆☆☆☆☆☆☆☆☆☆☆☆☆☆☆☆☆☆☆☆☆☆☆

To develop an attitude that will turn your life around, I believe one of the most important ingredients is *enthusiasm*. Persistence, ability, brains, and other attributes are important, but without enthusiasm, even the greatest ideas can become bogged down.

In his book, *How To Be a Winner in Selling,*[3] Hugh S. Bell gives the reader a five-point formula for developing the kind of enthusiasm that brings victory, the kind of enthusiasm that makes you a winner.

You want to improve your attitude? Bell says to *associate with enthusiastic people.* If we associate with people who are successful, we bring up our potential of being successful.

Let yourself get excited. The only place a poker face is an asset, Bell says, is in a poker game! Anywhere else, a display of approval, admiration, and enthusiasm are much better allies. When you are impressed with someone or something, let yourself show it. Get excited about it.

Bell writes, "Practice speaking so that what you have to say sounds important and exciting."

He suggests putting the same kind of excitement and enthusiasm into your profession that you would if you suddenly received a million-dollar inheritance.

However, it must be sincere enthusiasm. Without sincerity, your excitement lacks a foundation or real meaning. "Faking it" gives you a facade through which people see easily. Really believing in what you do sells. Without sincerity, success will not be yours.

One of the best ways to cultivate sincerity is to disassociate yourself from criticism and fault finding. There is a silver lining in every situation. Finding it creates happiness and enthusiasm.

☆ ☆

If you learn from a defeat, you haven't really lost. [4]

☆ ☆

Why not make this the day that you are going to decide, regardless of how you feel, that you will make a greater effort to be enthusiastic in your life?

This is not some kind of hype or an act where you cavort around yelling, "See how enthusiastic I am?"

Rather, I am talking about a sincere commitment to say:

"This is the day I am going to look on the bright side — the positive side — and I am going to try to find something positive and encouraging to say to everyone in every situation. I am going to make a commitment to have a new level of enthusiasm, to be an encourager of other people."

Ziglar says that we cannot tailor-make the situations of life, but we can tailor-make the attitudes to fit them before they arise.[5]

A positive attitude is like nourishment to the body and soul.

A right attitude can carry you through the worst days at work.

Negative attitudes are absolutely poisonous to the body. They actually lead to physical illnesses and emotional breakdowns.

✩ ✩

A merry heart doeth good like a medicine.
— Proverbs 17:22

✩ ✩

The body produces substances called *endorphins* that operate at different sites in the brain and spinal cord. They reduce the experience of pain and screen out unpleasant stimuli.

In fact, the presence of endorphins, which are secreted by the brain, actually causes a feeling of well-being.

Researchers today have learned that optimistic thoughts and positive attitudes can stimulate the production of endorphins.

Therefore, *we can simply choose our attitudes!*

Each of us are responsible for his or her attitude and mental outlook.

In business *or* ministry, the person with the ability to look on the bright side — the person with an optimistic outlook in life — establishes a camaraderie among fellow workers and helps to create an enthusiastic workplace.

You and I are in control of our attitudes. We cannot blame our bosses, our parents, or our spouses.

Charles Garfield says the attitudes and values of American business superstars are:[6]

1. They value achievement and find primary motivation through mission. [They value making a contribution and can take responsibility.]

2. They assist in the development of others.

3. They value self-development and pursue self-management through self-mastery. [They want to keep maturing through self-discipline.]

4. They value creativity and produce innovation through risk-taking. [They are not afraid to try something new.]

5. They look for points of alignment among the organizational team and personal objectives. [They look for ways in which their goals and the company's or ministry's goals match.]

6. They value quality and pay conscientious attention to feedback and course correction. [They wants things done right, listen to constructive criticism, and change accordingly.]

7. They value opportunity and meet the challenge of change. [They look for ways to improve and are not afraid or too dogmatic to change.]

Maintain a High Level of Motivation

Motivation furnishes a reason for commitment. This improves attitude. Motivation creates energy enough to carry you toward a worthwhile goal and to maintain the inner drive until that goal is accomplished.

Lack of motivation is the reason so few people achieve success — lack of motivation along with a poor attitude.

Eighty-four percent of American employees require constant supervision. Fourteen percent require *some* supervision. Only 2 percent work without supervision![7]

☆ ☆

If it is to be,
it is up to me.

☆ ☆

How we think and act is totally up to us. Looking for bad things to happen can actually cause them to come to pass. It is interesting that people with negative attitudes look for converts.

Because they expect situations such as losing a job, financial problems, poor relationships with others, unpleasant working conditions, and failures of all sorts — they try to convince other people that life is like that.

People who are success-oriented, people with good attitudes, can influence us to overcome significant obstacles.

If you really believe a goal can be reached, your attitude releases new energy that can help bring about the achievement.

If you would like to know your motivation and if this is causing an attitude problem, you may want to take the following test:[8]

Question No. 1: Do you constantly procrastinate on important tasks?

Question No. 2: Do you require coaxing to do small chores?

Question No. 3: Do you perform duties at your best, or just get by?

Question No. 4: Do you constantly talk negatively about your work?

Question No. 5: Do efforts of friends to enthuse you irritate you instead?

Question No. 6: Do you start small projects and leave them unfinished?

Question No. 7: Do you avoid self-improvement opportunities?

If you fall short, do not give up or get on a "guilt trip."

There are seven ways in which you can keep yourself motivated.[9] These things will improve your attitude until you can reach a turning point and begin to achieve your goal.

Seven Ways To Improve Motivation

1. *Know the value of enthusiasm and energy.*

Corporations pay millions of dollars each year for motivational seminars, incentive programs, and other special events to generate enthusiasm in their employees. They understand that motivated employees are productive employees.

They look for employees with winning attitudes. The force of motivation — a really good positive attitude — is the gasoline that fuels the fire until the task is completed. The optimistic approach brings a dream into reality.

☆☆☆☆☆☆☆☆☆☆☆☆☆☆☆☆☆☆☆☆☆☆☆☆

You are never defeated
as long as you don't think
the job is impossible.[10]

☆☆☆☆☆☆☆☆☆☆☆☆☆☆☆☆☆☆☆☆☆☆☆☆

2. *Evaluate the original reason you become motivated about a goal.*

53

Were your reasons personal — like pride of ownership or self-esteem?

Did you become energized by a dynamic speaker only to lose enthusiasm because you did not share his vision?

You cannot stay motivated for a dream in which you do not believe.

3. *Acknowledge the possibility of motivation limitations.*

Motivation can be limited or even destroyed if the integrity of the person, product, or philosophy associated with your efforts is questionable to you.

Your degree of motivation is only as high as your opinion of your goal. A lack of faith in your goal will quench your desire to succeed and paralyze your progress.

4. *Discern and appreciate the value of the cycles of motivation.*

Progress is not always measured by outward results.

☆ ☆

To every thing there is a season,
and a time to every purpose under the heaven.
— Ecclesiastes 3:1

☆ ☆

5. *Find the cause for your lack of motivation.*

Causes of lack of motivation can be found in spiritual, physical, emotional, financial, family support, or mental areas.

Once you find the cause, see what can be done to remove it or reduce it.

6. *Visualize the pain of failure and the rewards of accomplishment.*

Three basic motivations are desire for reward, punishment for failure, and self-esteem.

7. *Activate seven essential keys for maintaining motivation:*

• Confirmation,

• Concentration on goals,

• Renew your mind — tapes, books, and so forth,

• Information on how to reach the goal,

• Delegation of tasks,

• Associations (friends, relationships),

• Verbalization: Talk like a victor, not a victim.

> *The secret of winning is being able*
> *to get yourself going in the right direction*
> *and keep going*
> *until you get what you went after.* [11]
>
> — Mike Murdock

Endnotes

[1]Tan. *Encyclopedia,* p. 215, #552.

[2]Ziglar. *See You,* p. 204.

[3]Bell, Hugh S. *How To Be a Winner in Selling.* Copyright held by The Research and Review Service of America, Inc., 1720 E. 38th St., Indianapolis, IN 46218.

[4]Ziglar. p. 223.

[5]Ibid. p. 224.

[6]Excerpts from *Peak Performers* by Charles Garfield. Text copyright © 1986 by Charles Garfield, p. 266. Reprinted by permission of William Morrow and Co., Inc.

[7,8,9] Murdock. "Seven Ways To Stay Motivated," *A Mike Murdock Study Guide.*

[10]Carnegie, Dale. *Dale Carnegie's Scrapbook* (New York: Simon and Schuster 1959).

[11]Murdock. "Seven Ways."

Chapter 5
CONTROLLING YOUR ALARM SYSTEM

*I will lift up mine eyes
unto the hills,
from whence cometh my help.*

— Psalm 121:1

☆☆☆☆☆☆☆☆☆☆☆☆☆☆☆☆☆☆☆☆☆☆☆☆☆☆

Stress is the body's alarm system, part of our built-in defenses. When the "alarm" goes off, the body's systems are flooded with adrenal secretions. Normal activities are interrupted.

The heart beats faster. . .digestive juices begin to flow to speed up the fueling process. . .and hormones are released into the bloodstream.

The alarm system is preparing the body for physical action — for fight, attacking what is threatening us, or flight, running away. By taking action, the tension, or stress, is released.

If no action is taken, there is no release for the extra hormones that poured into the bloodstream. Dr. Archibald D. Hart compares the process to a rubber band: If it is stretched often enough, it loses its elasticity, "develops hairline cracks, and eventually snaps."[1]

At first, the body attempts to handle the situation by its other avenues of expression — sleeping and eating. You may find yourself suddenly very sleepy or very hungry.

☆☆☆☆☆☆☆☆☆☆☆☆☆☆☆☆☆☆☆☆☆☆☆☆

Hundreds of thousands of years ago,
this planet was populated by dinosaurs
the size of which we have not seen since.

Then something happened.
Scientists do not know for certain what.
But within a relatively short amount of time,
virtually all the gigantic beasts perished.
What scientists do agree on is. . .
dinosaurs could not adapt to the change.[2]

☆☆☆☆☆☆☆☆☆☆☆☆☆☆☆☆☆☆☆☆☆☆☆☆

Our defense systems work so well that most of the time, we are not even consciously aware of what is going on.

However, if the defense system breaks down, illness results.

Without expending the energy triggered by stress, the body reacts to overloaded systems with various ailments. The body cannot stand being under stress all the time.

Relieving stress is something that should be included in your plans to achieve a vision and goal.

Today, stress is an unavoidable fact of life. It is the result of events or changes in our lives, *stressors*. Not all of them are bad, but all of them carry a certain amount of stress. Stress results from promotion, marriage, having a child. Many times, stress helps us stay on our toes.

☆ ☆

The world breaks everyone and afterward many are strong at the broken places.[3]
— Ernest Hemingway

☆ ☆

Whether the effects are good or bad, stress is your alarm system. To achieve your vision and goal, you must understand stress and how it affects you personally and specifically. Problems arise when you experience a stress overload. Some people can handle more stress than others, which means it is impossible to predict exactly how much is too much. Also, your ability to cope with stress varies from day to day.

What Is Stress?

— You have four minutes to get to the bus stop, and you cannot find your wallet. *You are under stress.*

— Your electric bill arrived, and it was $50 higher than you expected; you just had to buy a new starter for the car, too. *You are under stress.*

— You are waiting to hear from the doctor about some tests you just had made. *You are under stress.*

Stress can be defined as the *rate of wear and tear on the body.*

It is any disruptive influence on a person, physical or psychological.

> Stress is anything that scares,
>   prods,
>   threatens,
>   thrills.

> Stress is anything that speeds up,
>   keys up, or
>   tenses up our bodies.

> Stress is anything that pushes us.

Everyone is under some type of stress every day. Without it, we would not move, get out of bed, or care about life.

We need it — but we do *not* need an excess of it.

In order to move from existing to living, from having no destination to having a vision and a goal, you must learn to deal with your alarm system — stress.

Physical stress involves an injury, a virus, a temperature change, having to expend energy in a way that is not customary: running if you are accustomed to a slow walk; standing a long time, if you usually sit.

Psychological stress is usually some threat to security, self-esteem, way of life, or safety — even an argument with your spouse or reprimand from the boss.

A threat of any kind produces fear, especially the fear of loss. Another major fear is uncertainty of any kind, and the greatest cause of uncertainty is *change*.

☆ ☆

Life today creates greater stresses than that of previous times. This is because there is much less stability, much less agreement as to standards. Emphasis on the individual and on individual decision-making (conscience) increases the pressures and uncertainties that foster stress.

☆ ☆

Your alarm system has a cycle of three stages:

Alarm is the first stage, when you first become aware of a change or an event coming at you, a "happening" with which you must deal.

Activation is the point at which all of the body systems are affected. Many times, you will feel great at this stage. You are into an adrenaline "high." You feel "in control," as if you can handle anything.

Recovery occurs after the situation is over. Suddenly, you feel tired and sleepy, or tired and hungry. The surge of adrenaline has stopped, and the body lets down.

Unfortunately, many of us have many chances a day for this automatic cycle to occur. Most of us do not know how it works, or even when it is operating. In order to achieve your vision and goal in good health, it is imperative to learn to cooperate with your alarm system.

✩ ✩

Adrenaline arousal can be compared to revving up an engine and then leaving it to idle. Idling an engine on high for a short period of time clears out gum deposits and dirty carbon. But when the engine is left idling for a long time, carbon deposits collect in the valves. The engine wears out faster. [4]

✩ ✩

As you move toward a turning point in your life, you need to begin to look for signs of stress in your life. Here are some common signs of stress:

• Tense muscles; sore neck, shoulders, and back, and possibly, headaches and cramps.

• Insomnia — including difficulty falling asleep or sleeping all night; also waking up too early.

• Fatigue not caused by physical exertion.

• Boredom, listlessness, dullness, lack of interest.

• Drinking too much, or increased use of medications.

• Eating too much, or too little.

• Diarrhea, cramps, "gas," constipation, or menstrual irregularities.

• Heart skips or palpitations.

• Phobias.

• Tics, restlessness, or itching.

☆☆☆☆☆☆☆☆☆☆☆☆☆☆☆☆☆☆☆☆☆☆☆☆☆

Thou wilt keep him in perfect peace,
whose mind is stayed on thee:
because he trusteth in thee.

— Isaiah 26:3

☆☆☆☆☆☆☆☆☆☆☆☆☆☆☆☆☆☆☆☆☆☆☆☆☆

Man is so constructed that the obvious dangers and visible threats are easier to deal with than the invisible, illusive, or embarrassing day-to-day irritants.

T. H. Holmes and R. H. Rahe have devised a test that will give you a better handle on the amount of stress in your life from normal or ordinary events — not counting the emergencies or extraordinary occurrences.[5]

Stress Test

Death of Spouse:	100
Divorce:	73
Marital Separation:	65
Jail Term:	63
Death of Close Family Member:	63
Personal Injury or Illness:	53
Marriage:	50
Fired at Work:	47
Marital Reconciliation:	45
Retirement:	43

Pregnancy:	40
Sex Difficulties:	39
New Family Member:	39
Business Readjustment:	39
Change in Financial Status:	38
Death of a Close Friend:	37
Change to Different Line of Work:	36
Change in Number of Arguments With Spouse:	35
Mortgage Over $10,000:	31
Foreclosure:	30
Child Leaving Home:	29
Trouble With In-Laws:	29
Outstanding Personal Achievement:	28
Wife Begins or Stops Work:	26
Beginning or Ending of School:	26
Trouble With the Boss:	23
Change in Residence:	20
Change in Schools:	20
Mortgage, or Loan Less Than $10,000:	17
Change in Number of Family Get-Togethers:	15
Christmas:	12

300 or more points in one year = exceptionally high risk for the development of some stress-related problems.

225-299, high risk;

150-244, medium risk;

150 or less, low risk.

Obviously, some of these stressors cannot be avoided; therefore, the way to deal with your alarm system is to learn to control it, once you understand how it functions in you.

Charles Garfield says:

"True peak performers, while capable of intense effort, retain an ability to relax that allows them to keep sight of results, long-range outcome, pacing, flexibility, and the importance of self-renewal."[6]

How do you deal with what Archibald D. Hart calls the "hurry sickness" or "adrenaline addiction"? Hart has listed these tips for reducing stress:[7]

1. *Talk audibly to yourself.*

Tell yourself to calm down, to quit acting as if life were a 100-yard dash. Remind yourself that you are just a part of a bigger whole. If you will stop playing Messiah, you will have considerably less stress.

2. *Practice conscious physical relaxation.*

You must allow your body to unwind so that healing and restoration can take place. One way is to exercise regularly. Exercise can not only improve your physical health, but also your prayer life, mood, and general feeling of well-being.

But remember that exercise can build tension or release it. Aerobics is good, but pushing yourself too far in the reduction of stress simply adds more stress!

3. *Remember that frantic behavior does not guarantee success.*

4. Ask yourself, *Is the price I must pay* (in the situation, whatever it is) *really worth the benefit?*

5. *Learn to deliberately slow down.*

6. *Quickly resolve those emotions that are adrenaline "biggies."*

These include anger, resentment, frustration, irritation, and excitement. Here are three "sure cures" for such adrenaline triggers:

Apologize if you are wrong.
Bury hurts due to insensitivity.
Forgive hurts due to others' insensitivity.

7. *Review your vision and goal*

Consider whether God would want you to "burnout" in your quest for success.

8. *Look closely at the faces of those around you.*

Do they seem like friends or foes?

Are you forgetting they also are people?

Have you slowed down enough to really understand your children? Do everyone a favor by easing up on your demands on yourself and them.

9. *Relax your expectations, and enjoy the world around you.*

☆☆☆☆☆☆☆☆☆☆☆☆☆☆☆☆☆☆☆☆☆☆☆

Edwin R. Roberts of Princeton Seminary once sat under a pastor who concluded his announcements: "I am not going to take a vacation this summer, the devil never does!"

Roberts went home and re-read the Gospels to see what Jesus' attitude is. He found that of His three years of active ministry, there were mentioned 10 periods of retirement! This was in addition to the nightly rest and sabbath rest.

Whose example are we following? the devil's?[8]

☆☆☆☆☆☆☆☆☆☆☆☆☆☆☆☆☆☆☆☆☆☆☆

Two guidelines for reducing stress are:

• To recognize stress for what it is.

• To understand how it works.

Ways of Reducing Stress

For many people, building faith in the Word of God, faith in their relationship with Jesus, and a consistent prayer life will help to reduce stress.

Fellowship with a group of people who can provide support.

For some, a more personal, specific approach may be necessary. One way is to avoid stress-producing situations. This is not always possible, but many stressors *can* be avoided:

1. *Environmental stress* — excessive noise, crowded conditions, or heavy traffic could be reduced with a little planning and awareness.

A change of job or change of attitude toward a job may be in order.

Recognizing economic or political forces beyond your control helps keep you from trying to lift weights too heavy for you.

Reevaluating your talents, abilities, and goals can be helpful.

☆ ☆

Learn to avoid "avoidable stress." Try to avoid too many big changes in your life at the same time.

☆ ☆

2. *Learn to relax.*

John Savage, the great insurance man with Columbus Mutual, said that people need to work eight hours and play eight hours — they just need to make sure it is not the same eight hours!

One way to relax tense muscles is to tighten them more, and then let go. Try stretching out or taking a short nap during the day, if it is at all possible.

☆ ☆

Some seek bread;
and some seek wealth and ease;
and some seek fame,
but all are seeking rest. [9]
— Frederick Langbridge

☆ ☆

Fresh air supplies extra oxygen, especially when combined with deep breathing brought on by exercise. If you are tired after work, and your job is sedentary, try taking a walk.

Join a health club and get involved in racquetball, jogging, or some other positive, consistent exercise program rather than grabbing a soft drink and something to eat immediately after sitting all day.

3. *Accepting what cannot be changed is a great help!*

☆ ☆

Control what you can control.
Accept what you cannot control.
Learn the difference between the two.

☆ ☆

4. *Eat properly, do not rush or skip meals, and maintain a balanced diet.*

5. *Plan your activities to use time and energy efficiently.*

6. *Engage in hobbies, or other recreations.*

A hobby should be something different from the work you do all day long and should be fun!

7. *Communicate your problems to others: family, friends, pastor or counselors.*

8. *Provide service to others.* Using your skills and leisure time to help others takes you out of yourself. A doctor named Luke wrote down these words of Jesus:

> *Give, and it shall be given unto you. . . .*
> — Luke 6:38

9. *Get enough sleep.* Along with enough rest during the day, keeping the body's alarm system operating properly requires enough sleep at night.

I will both lay me down in peace, and sleep; for thou, Lord, only makest me dwell in safety.

— Psalm 4:8

If you have a problem going to sleep, try thinking about beautiful and hopeful things, good things that have happened to you.

If you are a Christian, pray instead of counting sheep. Meditating on some of the Psalms, such as the twenty-third, also can bring the mind into rest — and when the mind is at rest, the body soon follows suit.

☆ ☆

What you get by reaching your destination isn't nearly as important as what you become by reaching that destination. [10]

— Zig Ziglar

☆ ☆

10. *Love and do not hate.* Intense emotions, such as hate, anger, resentment, fear, or bitterness also "rev up" the engine of the body's alarm system. They cause acid secretions to be thrown into the other systems.

Love and forgiveness are for *your* benefit more than the other person's. Love is the greatest weapon of self-defense that exists.

Love is a choice,
a decision,
a set of characteristic behaviors (1 Cor. 13),
an action.

Love is not a feeling.
"Feelings" are a result of love,
or of lust.
It is a deception to mistake feelings for attitude.

☆☆☆☆☆☆☆☆☆☆☆☆☆☆☆☆☆☆☆☆☆☆

Do It Anyway

People are unreasonable, illogical, and self-centered.
Love them anyway.
If you do good, you will be accused of selfish motives.
Do good anyway.
Success will win you false friends and true enemies.
Succeed anyway.
The good you do today will be forgotten tomorrow.
Do good anyway.
Honesty and frankness cause you to be vulnerable.
Be honest and frank anyway.
The biggest people with the biggest ideas can be shot
down by the smallest people with the smallest ideas.
Think big anyway.
People favor underdogs but follow topdogs.
Fight for some underdog anyway.
What you spend years building may be destroyed overnight.
Build anyway.
People need help but may attack you if you try.
Help them anyway.

Giving the world the best you have may get you kicked in the teeth. *Give the world your best anyway.* [11]

— Author Unknown

Endnotes

[1]Hart, Dr. Archibald D. *The Hidden Link Between Adrenalin and Stress* (Texas: Waco, Word Books. Copyright © 1986 by Archibald D. Hart), p. 23.

[2]Waitley. *Joy*, p. 117.

[3]Hemingway, Ernest. *A Farewell to Arms.* Quoted in Garfield's *Peak Performers*, p. 164.

[4]Hart. *The Hidden Link*, p. 38, 39.

[5]Homes, T. H., Rahe, R. H. *The Social Readjustment Scale.*

[6]Garfield. *Peak Performers*, p. 228.

[7]Hart. "Addicted to Adrenalin," *Focus on the Family*, Arcadia, California 91006, April 1986, pp. 7, 15.

[8]Tan. *Encyclopedia*, p. 1139, #5003.

[9]Edwards, Tryon; editor. *The New Dictionary of Thoughts* (Standard Book Company, 1960), p. 570.

[10]Ziglar. *See You at the Top*, p. 244.

[11]Read by Julius Irving, "Dr. J.", at a banquet.

Chapter 6
WORDS ARE
KEYS TO SUCCESS

Words are both better and worse than thoughts;
they express them, and add to them;
they give them power for good or evil;
they start them on an endless flight,
for instruction and comfort and blessing,
or for injury, sorrow and ruin. [1]

— Tryon Edwards

✩✩✩✩✩✩✩✩✩✩✩✩✩✩✩✩✩✩✩✩✩✩✩✩✩

Words are the most powerful things in the universe.

The words we speak will either hold us in bondage or bring us into success. Many people have been held captive in their circumstances by their own words.

If you are not already moving toward victory in your life, and you want to turn things around — "to stay in the game" — you will need to change your vocabulary.

There is a little rhyme that used to be heard often on school playgrounds:

> "Sticks and stones may break my bones,
> but names (words) will never hurt me."

However cute that may sound, or however defiant to those doing the name-calling, it is not true. Names and words either put us over in life or they hurt us.

Words Are Either Creative or Destructive.

The following kinds of statements hold you in bondage to the past and the present:

- I will never be able to have that, or afford that.

- We never have enough money.

- That scared me to death.

- We always catch everything that is going around.

- I am not smart enough to do that.

- I cannot do anything about my temper (laziness, crankiness, or whatever), because I get it from my father or grandfather. I am just like him.

They predispose you to give up trying to be different; they reflect what you believe; as a Christian, words like these are negative faith. With these kinds of statements and these kinds of beliefs, you are speaking death to yourself and your future instead of life. There is no hope in those words, no belief that things can ever be different.

☆☆☆☆☆☆☆☆☆☆☆☆☆☆☆☆☆☆☆☆☆☆☆☆

As you believe, so do you speak; and as you speak, so do you act; as you act, so goes your future.

☆☆☆☆☆☆☆☆☆☆☆☆☆☆☆☆☆☆☆☆☆☆☆☆

Words Made a Difference in My Life

In my own life, if I had spoken those kinds of words, I might be working in a filling station somewhere in Pennsylvania instead of being able to help others through *words* of motivation and encouragement.

In high school, I had not applied myself to study, being too interested in pranks and fun. The result was that I caused problems and did not get along with my teachers. Yet, I never got away from a hope for a good future.

In fact, my reputation was so bad that when I went back to my old high school some years after graduation and introduced myself to a former teacher as "Van Crouch," she said:

"You couldn't be. He's supposed to be in prison."

Academically, I was in the third of my class that made the upper two-thirds possible!

When I went to the guidance counselor about going to college, she said:

"Van, we have a lot of young men in this school who don't *know* what's going on in life, but you don't even *suspect* anything!"

Seriously, there were a lot of strikes against my ever making anything out of myself.

The things I am telling you in this book are things that I personally have used and know work. I know from my own experience that the words you speak make a lot of difference.

Rather than speak words of discouragement and failure, if I cannot speak something positive, I have found that humor bridges the gap. Seeing the humorous side of things enables me to make a quip, a "one-liner" at myself or circumstances.

It makes me feel better about myself and situations and usually lifts the spirits of those around me.

Words that will help you do not have to be serious or dramatic, *but they must be true to life* and they must be positive — filled with life, not death.

My life now is spent in the use of words to help others. I could not do that, if I had not learned to use words to encourage, edify, and strengthen myself.

I can truthfully tell you from my own experience that the words you speak about yourself and your circumstances literally can change things. They can make the difference between defeat and success.

Remember that your attitude sets or confirms your vision? *Words* determine your attitude.

☆☆☆☆☆☆☆☆☆☆☆☆☆☆☆☆☆☆☆☆☆☆☆

Many a treasure besides Ali Baba's
is unlocked with a verbal key.[2]
— Henry Van Dyke

☆☆☆☆☆☆☆☆☆☆☆☆☆☆☆☆☆☆☆☆☆☆☆

Solomon said in Proverbs 6:2:

"Thou art snared by the words of thy mouth."

Words filled with optimism, with hope, with belief that, in this country, a man can be everything he *can* be, will shape a positive future for you.

Speech filled with fear, doubt, unbelief, and negativism can cause defeat in your life.

You must *believe what you say.*

You must develop faith in your words in order to believe that what you are saying day after day will come to pass.

In other words, the old adage, "If you cannot say something good, don't say anything at all," is a good rule to live by!

Not "Magic," but Common Sense

How to talk is important.

Talking about the importance of words in your life does not mean there is any "magic" in words themselves.

I am not implying any sort of "flaky," weird formula, such as "open sesame."[3] However, words *are* "verbal keys."

There *is* power in your words simply because you believe whatever you say.

Whatever you believe is how you begin to do things in life.

If you have been told by parents or teachers that you are "dumb," that *word* will shape your future because you begin to *believe* it. Then you will not try to do anything that takes mental effort.

Spoken words "program" your heart for either success or defeat. Little by little, you *can* change things in your life, which will change your future. Positive words are like the rudder on a ship. They can turn it in another direction.

Zig Ziglar tells a story in his book, *See You at the Top*, that illustrates this perfectly.

Three Little Girls

"One day, a friend of mine in the insurance business stopped by (my office) for a visit. He brought his three daughters who were about three, five, and seven years of age. They were dressed in pretty dresses and looked like little dolls.

"Incredibly enough, he introduced them this way: 'This is the one who won't eat, this is the one who won't mind her mother, and this is the one who cries all the time.'

"There is no question in my mind about this man's love for those three little ones. It showed all over his face and in his eyes as he petted and played with them. Unfortunately, he was giving them something 'to live down to.' The way he saw them was the way he was treating them.

"He was giving powerful, negative instructions to each one."[4]

America in the later part of the 20th century is an extremely negative society. One hundred years ago, there was an atmosphere of hope, an upbeat attitude in society, that is not there today. People's words were full of hope for the future. The input from all forms of the media today is based on the premise that "good news is not news."

If you grew up in a home environment where much of your input also was negative, it is doubly hard today for you to overcome that word-conditioning. With twenty or more years in a negative environment, your thinking is not going to turn around overnight.

☆☆☆☆☆☆☆☆☆☆☆☆☆☆☆☆☆☆☆☆☆☆☆☆

No man has a prosperity so high or firm,
but that two or three words can dishearten it;
and there is no calamity
which right words will not begin to redress.[5]
— Ralph Waldo Emerson

☆☆☆☆☆☆☆☆☆☆☆☆☆☆☆☆☆☆☆☆☆☆☆☆

The key is not to get discouraged. It *can* be done. Others have overcome such odds, and so can you.

The starting point is to begin to "reprogram" your mind, and that takes time.

The way to "reprogram" is to begin to speak words of encouragement and belief in yourself *to* yourself:

- I *can* achieve my goal.

- I *can* be more than I am right now.

- I *can* be free of the negativism of the past.

- I *do* live in a country of great opportunities.

- I *can* be whatever I set myself to be.

- I *will* achieve my vision and my goal.

To see your situation changed, you need to begin to speak the desired result.

Operate at Your Own Level

A good principle to apply here is, "Operate at your own level."

If you start out by setting your microgoal (the next fifteen minutes) as becoming the president of United Airlines, then you are going to fail, no matter how much you speak the words, "I will be the president of United Airlines."

Do not set yourself up for more failure by unreasonable words.

Words to establish a better microgoal would be:

"I will not speak negative words about myself or others for the next fifteen minutes," or, "I will speak positive words for the next fifteen minutes."

Another principle is this:

Words are no substitute for hard work and perseverance.

☆ ☆

> *Words should be employed as the means,*
> *not as the end;*
> *language is the instrument,*
> *conviction is the work.*[6]
> — Sir Joshua Reynolds

☆ ☆

Simply because you have started to understand the importance of words, do not throw good business principles down the drain!

Also, do not be too hasty in your words. Consider your speech well, because your words do direct your life.

☆☆☆☆☆☆☆☆☆☆☆☆☆☆☆☆☆☆☆☆☆☆☆

Volatility of words is carelessness in acts;
words are the wings of action. [7]
— John Caspar Lavater

☆☆☆☆☆☆☆☆☆☆☆☆☆☆☆☆☆☆☆☆☆☆☆☆

Endnotes

[1] *The New Dictionary of Thoughts,* p. 739.

[2] Ibid.

[3] The magic words spoken to open the door to the treasure in "Ali Baba and the Forty Thieves."

[4] Ziglar, *See You,* p. 121.

[5] *The New Dictionary,* p. 739.

[6] Ibid.

[7] Ibid.

Chapter 7

ALL RUNNERS RUN, BUT ONLY ONE GETS THE PRIZE

The common denominator of success lies in forming the habit of doing things that failures don't like to do.[1]

— Albert E. N. Gray

☆☆☆☆☆☆☆☆☆☆☆☆☆☆☆☆☆☆☆☆☆☆☆☆

You are in a race whether you want to be or not.

In a race, all runners run, but only one gets the prize.

Run in such a way as to get the prize.

Once you decide that you want to be the one who wins, the one who gets the prize, then you have another question:

"How do I maintain what I have until I obtain the prize?"

Here are ten principles that will help you:

1. Work Hard.

Pursue work compatible with your interests — your vision and goal — and with your abilities and talents.

☆☆☆☆☆☆☆☆☆☆☆☆☆☆☆☆☆☆☆☆☆☆☆

Never try to teach a pig to sing.
It wastes your time and annoys the pig.

☆☆☆☆☆☆☆☆☆☆☆☆☆☆☆☆☆☆☆☆☆☆☆

Albert E. N. Gray, former president of Prudential Insurance Co., wrote a booklet called, "The Common Denominator of Success."

In it, he said that successful people do the things other people do not like to do. Also, he pointed out that those people who only do what they like and do not want to spend time on tasks that are tedious, boring, or strenuous usually are the people who fail at life.

✩ ✩

Work is a four-letter word,
but it is not a dirty word.

✩ ✩

2. Never Give Up.

The moment you decide to have a turning point in your life, you will have some great opportunities to quit, to throw in the towel, to give up, to say, "It's not worth it."

But there is a difference between quitting and wanting to quit. Just because you want to quit — which is natural — does not mean you *have* to quit.

Someone has said, "No pain, no gain."

When I was young, I had pains in my legs. I would go to my mother and say, "Mom, what are these pains I am having?"

And she would say, "Those are just 'growing pains.' You are getting stronger. You are going to be able to run faster. You are going to be able to jump higher. You are going to be able to perform better in sports."

My mother's words became *positive forces* in my life.

3. Learn To Enjoy the Climb.

Striving for success is like climbing a mountain.

It is great to reach the top, but learn to enjoy the climb.

There are some things that will happen during a mountain climb:

- You will be stretched.

- You will be pulled.

- You will run out of breath and have an opportunity to quit or to stick to your goal.

- You will learn how to pace yourself for the long haul.

It is in the climb, not in reaching the top, that you are developed.

You may have great talent, but without character development or the developing of skills, you may not be able to build that talent into a successful career.

4. Prepare for Tomorrow.

One of the ways to prepare for tomorrow is to develop a vision and a goal, as we discussed in the first two chapters.

Next, after you have dealt with your attitude, your ability to handle stress, and your habit of speaking negative words, you need to begin to get involved in continuing education.

☆☆☆☆☆☆☆☆☆☆☆☆☆☆☆☆☆☆☆☆☆☆☆

> The immature mind hops from one thing
> to another;
> the mature mind seeks to follow through.[2]
> — Harry A. Overstreet

☆☆☆☆☆☆☆☆☆☆☆☆☆☆☆☆☆☆☆☆☆☆☆

The 20th century has been called "the information age," and basic knowledge is increasing so rapidly that the understanding and interpretation of that knowledge is lagging far behind. We are overwhelmed with data.

The point for us as individuals is that in our chosen fields of endeavor, what we know now probably will be obsolete in five years — or less.

5. Never Be Embarrassed To Ask for Help.

Ben Feldman, a great insurance salesman — still selling at seventy-seven — for the New York Life Insurance Company, said:

"Only a fool learns by his own experiences."

We can all learn from other people, especially those who have succeeded in the fields that we have chosen.

Look for constructive criticism. Assume that people around you may have some insights into you that you do not have.

✩✩✩✩✩✩✩✩✩✩✩✩✩✩✩✩✩✩✩✩✩✩✩✩

God has so ordered that men,
being in need of each other,
should learn to love each other,
and bear each other's burdens. [3]
— George Augustus Sala

✩✩✩✩✩✩✩✩✩✩✩✩✩✩✩✩✩✩✩✩✩✩✩✩

It is important to reach to others if you need help. Do not try to "go it alone."

Find help if you need it.

6. Find a Hero, a "Role Model."

Successful people leave footprints in the sand.

Find successful people with whom to associate.

Jim Sundberg, the great catcher now with the Texas Rangers ball team, calls this his "life board of directors."

☆☆☆☆☆☆☆☆☆☆☆☆☆☆☆☆☆☆☆☆☆☆☆☆

Without counsel purposes are disappointed:
but in the multitude of counselors
they are established.

— Proverbs 15:22

☆☆☆☆☆☆☆☆☆☆☆☆☆☆☆☆☆☆☆☆☆☆☆☆

Then find someone to pattern your life after, someone who exemplifies excellence in some form in his, or her, life. Watch how this person acts and works and speaks. Then apply those principles to your own life.

I am not saying to "copy" someone's personality, but to appropriate whatever characteristics have contributed to their success.

☆☆☆☆☆☆☆☆☆☆☆☆☆☆☆☆☆☆☆☆☆☆☆☆

Every man is a hero and an oracle to somebody,
and to that person, whatever he says
has an enhanced value. [4]

— Ralph Waldo Emerson

☆☆☆☆☆☆☆☆☆☆☆☆☆☆☆☆☆☆☆☆☆☆☆☆

7. Be a Leader.

A leader is not a title. . .it is not a particular type of personality. . .a leader is someone who goes ahead and does what has to be done *before* it has to be done.

A good leader does not spread garbage (speak evil) about another. Look for the good in a person. Project an attitude of forgiveness. Give favor to people, and you will reap favor.

Do more than is expected of you.

☆ ☆

The great difference between the real (leader) and the pretender is, that the one sees into the future, while the other regards only the present; the one lives by the day, and acts on expediency; the other acts on enduring principles and for immortality. [5]

— Edmund Burke

☆ ☆

Everyone can be a leader in something.

You can have expertise in one particular area of knowledge. Set a standard for others around you.

Remember, however, that people have a right to higher expectations of you when you decide to move out and be a leader.

8. Set Priorities.

Drift, drown, or decide.

Eliminate procrastination, maintain momentum, and you will get the job done.

Be accountable to somebody.

Dr. R. Henry Migliore, college professor, author, and industry consultant, lists several things in his book, *Personal Action Planning,*[6] that will help you set your priorities:

• How will you get there (to your vision and goal)?

• List four things you must do in the next few months to get where you want to be next year, and in five years.

• List four things that are holding you back.

• How can you overcome each of those obstacles?

• Whose help do you need to achieve your potential and get where you want to be in five years?

9. Be Yourself.

If I could not play but one note on the piano, I would want it to be natural, to be *my* note.

I want to be myself as God intended me to be.

☆ ☆

It is better to die with a good name,
than to live with a bad one.[7]
— Malay Proverb

☆ ☆

10. Forget Past Mistakes

You *can* learn from past mistakes, but there is no point in spending a lot of time looking back unless that is the direction you want to go!

You cannot unscramble eggs.

Learn to go on.

Press toward the goal.

Ten Pitfalls That Can Stall Your Career

As you move forward toward your goal, perhaps there will come a time when suddenly you are stalled, when things seem to be at a standstill, when you do not seem to be going anywhere, much less ahead.

What do you do then?

You begin to take inventory.

You analyze what is happening to find the cause and the solution.

Here are ten things Mark McCormack, author and chairman of International Management Group, says that he has seen stall the careers of even the ablest executives, even though they were very good at what they were doing.[8]

1. *Not knowing why you were hired.*
   McCormack says the main reason anyone is hired is: "to make the boss look better."

2. *Following up too slowly.*
   "Failure to act immediately on a boss's command lingers in the boss's mind and usually taints your reputation."

3. *Ignoring the Peter Principle.*
   This "principle" is that everyone eventually rises to his, or her, level of incompetence. If you promote someone who has no interest in the job you are promoting him to, this principle will begin to operate; and, if you allow yourself to be promoted to a position that you know you have no desire for, this will begin to operate in your life.

☆☆☆☆☆☆☆☆☆☆☆☆☆☆☆☆☆☆☆☆☆☆☆

Street-stupid executives reach their level of incompetence faster than they should.
— McCormack

☆☆☆☆☆☆☆☆☆☆☆☆☆☆☆☆☆☆☆☆☆☆☆

If you are stalled, examine yourself and circumstances carefully to see if this is the problem.

4. *Ignoring the corporate culture.*
Do not seek the spotlight if you are in a "team" culture. Do not work eight-hour days, if everyone else is putting in twelve-hour days. The best way to be a non-conformist is to out-perform everyone else, McCormack says.

5. *Wanting to be liked by everyone.*
"Decisions should be dictated by the *situation* not by your sympathies and personal feelings." Everyone is *not* going to like you. That is an unrealistic expectation.

6. *Failing to cooperate when a new boss appears.*

7. *Going public with your private thoughts.*
Do not gossip about others at work, and do not share too many intimate thoughts and facts about yourself and your own life.

8. *Behaving inconsistently.*

Blowing up one day over something, and the next day, letting something you need to deal with go by will not build confidence in your bosses, peers, or subordinates!

9. *Blaming bad news on someone else.*

There is no harm in admitting you made a mistake. If you are making too many, something else is wrong that you need to examine; however, do not blame your errors on someone else. Sooner or later, you will be found out.

10. *Asking employees to do something you will not do yourself.*

Another point that will save you much trouble is: *Keep accurate records.*

Whether you are dealing with the Internal Revenue Service or stockholders or whoever you are responsible to, honest, accurate records can do nothing but help.

One more thing you need to consider:

Winning is important, but there is one thing that may cost you the prize: wrong motives.

One of the best pieces of advice along this line that I know of was written by John Brodie, former quarterback for the San Francisco 49ers:

You play to win.

There's no doubt about that.

But if winning is your first and only aim, you stand a good chance of losing.

You have the greatest chance of winning when your first commitment is to a total and enthusiastic involvement in the game itself.

Enthusiasm is what matters most.

If I was enthusiastic about the game, enjoying it, and doing my absolute best, then I had the best chance of winning it.

But then I could also handle losing, because I had done my best.

If you can't handle losing, you'll never be a big winner.

It is never easy to lose.

But if I knew I had performed at the top of my ability, with total involvement, that would take care of the winning or the losing.

The desire to be number one can be very dangerous.

If being number one is your first motive, you always end up stepping on someone else to get there, which means you can't ever really enjoy the accomplishments of someone else playing the same position. You can't enjoy his performance because you are always watching to see if he's better than you are.

The goal, it seems to me, is to be as good as you can be.

If this makes you number one, fine.

If not, you haven't lost anything, and you have gained a lot.

You can enjoy what others do.

You can respect the qualities that are involved in doing the job.

You can really wish the other guy well.

It is awfully lonely being number one, if you have had to fight your way upward through a pecking order with that goal in mind.

Out on the golf links, where I have spent a good deal of my time, I found the best players are also guys who root for the other guy's shot.

This kind of player enjoys the game; he enjoys all the qualities involved in the participation of it.

He is not rooting against his own shot; he still wants to win.

But the more positive energy you bring to the field, the better your own chances are.[9]

Brodie was writing about sports, but the same principles will bring excellence in your career.

It is kind of a cliche today in the business world that *good help is hard to find*. But if you want excellence in your career and in your life, you will take a job and do more than is expected of you.

Brodie mentioned something that Cliff C. Jones, chairman of Jones and Babson, Inc., agrees is "the decisive element in the formula for success": *enthusiasm*.

Jones' quoted some well-known people on enthusiasm in *Winning Through Integrity*, some quotes I would like to use to end this chapter:[10]

You can do anything if you have enthusiasm .... Enthusiasm is at the bottom of all progress.

With it, there is accomplishment. Without it, there are only alibis (Henry Ford).

Enthusiasm is the propelling force that is necessary for climbing the ladder of success (B. C. Forbes).

Nothing great was ever achieved without enthusiasm (Ralph Waldo Emerson).

No man who is enthusiastic about his work has anything to fear from life (Samuel Goldwyn).

Endnotes

[1]Gray, Albert E. N. "The Common Denominator of Success." Prudential Insurance Company of America.

[2]*The New Dictionary of Thought,* p. 407

[3]Ibid., p. 269.

[4]Ibid., pp. 269, 270.

[5]Ibid., p. 638

[6]Migliore, R. Henry. *Personal Action Planning* (Tulsa: Honor Books. Copyright © 1988 by R. Henry Migliore), pp. 39, 41.

[7]*Encyclopedia of 7700 Illustrations,* p. 1139, #5002.

[8]"Ten Pitfalls That Can Stall Your Career," From Mark McCormack's *Success Secrets* Newsletter.

[9]Brodie, John. *Openfield,* Human Resource Institute, Inc., 790 Frontage Road, Northfield, Illinois 60093.

[10]Jones, Cliff C. *Winning Through Integrity* (Nashville: Abingdon Press, 1985), pp. 103, 104.

Chapter 8
IT'S TIME TO GET ORGANIZED

*Organizational ability is often even more important
than intelligence in getting ahead.* [1]
— Beveridge and Davidson

☆☆☆☆☆☆☆☆☆☆☆☆☆☆☆☆☆☆☆☆☆☆☆☆

Up to this point, my emphasis has been on attitudes, concepts, and principles, i.e. *intangibles.* Now let us talk about some *tangibles.*

One of the most important is the ability to organize. Whether it is material, tasks, or people, knowing how to arrange things by order — priority to do, importance of material, or whatever else is involved, is half the task. Some things are common denominators to all organizational systems:[2]

1. Prioritize your activities.

2. Stick to the plan.

3. Think and organize in terms of departments (or categories).

4. If you feel overwhelmed, get out!

Also, do not get discouraged if organizing does not come naturally to you. There are many aids available, as well as books detailing methods of organizing that you can adopt.

If you sometimes fail and *do* get discouraged, consider this guy:

☆☆☆☆☆☆☆☆☆☆☆☆☆☆☆☆☆☆☆☆☆☆☆☆

He dropped out of grade school.

Ran a country store. Went broke. Took 15 years to pay off his bills.

Took a wife. Unhappy marriage until his death.

Ran for the U. S. House of Representatives. Lost twice. Ran for the U. S. Senate. Lost twice.

Delivered a speech to an indifferent audience, yet it became a classic.

Was attacked daily by the press and despised by
half the country.

Despite all this, imagine how many people all over
the world have been inspired by this awkward,
rumpled, brooding man who signed his name
simply
...A. Lincoln.[3]

☆☆☆☆☆☆☆☆☆☆☆☆☆☆☆☆☆☆☆☆☆☆☆☆

Most of us think that unless we have high I. Q.s, good
educations, and a lot of experience, we cannot become
leaders in our fields. However, Beveridge and Davidson
point out that many people who make it big in the business
world do *not* have:

- High intelligence quotients,

- Great experience in their fields.

- Advanced or intensive formal educations.

As the quote above shows, Abraham Lincoln certainly
had none of those three things.

Some great achievers in any field, of course, are well-
educated, very intelligent, and have experience, but in-depth
investigations into their backgrounds will show that other

factors were more involved in their success — factors such as:

- being able to organize material and time,

- having visions and goals,

- being determined to persevere until they reach their goals.

What success I have had in my present field of motivating, exhorting, and encouraging others certainly could not be attributed to my great intellect, great experience before entering this field, or to formal education.

Whenever I graduated, it was not *magna cum laude,* but " 'Lawdie,' how come?"

I graduated college in four terms — those of Kennedy, Johnson, Nixon, and Ford!

My motivational experience had been confined to cheering my favorite teams on to victory.

Beveridge and Davidson say they would select someone with good organizational skills over someone with twenty years experience who cannot organize and over someone who can speak eloquently but cannot organize.

☆ ☆

Organizational skills are always
cornerstones of business success. [4]

☆ ☆

It Pays To Organize

In addition to being considered by management consultants as necessary to success, putting things in proper order contributes to your morale, your sense of well-being. Being organized makes it easier for you to deal with several things at once and to handle the crises that develop in any business or career.

Being organized is profitable.

Some of the components of organization also can be used in your personal life to help bring discipline into it. Remember: behind every successful man is a surprised mother-in-law!

There may be exceptions to the rule where organization is concerned.

There may be successful businessmen whose desks are cluttered and who do not keep detailed lists or files.

However, you will find that those men usually have things organized in their heads. They know where everything is in the midst of seeming clutter.

For those of us without the kinds of memories necessary to operate this way, we must substitute lists, desk diaries, and filing systems.

The important thing is that becoming successful requires the recognition that organization is necessary in some form of expression or another.

☆☆☆☆☆☆☆☆☆☆☆☆☆☆☆☆☆☆☆☆☆☆☆☆

Order is a lovely nymph,
the child of beauty and wisdom;
Her attendants are comfort, neatness, and activity;
her abode is the valley of happiness:

She is always to be found when sought for,
and never appears so lovely
as when contrasted with her opponent,
disorder. [5]

— Samuel Johnson

☆☆☆☆☆☆☆☆☆☆☆☆☆☆☆☆☆☆☆☆☆☆☆☆

We have a pianist in our church who plays "Biblical" piano; in other words, her right hand does not know what her left hand is doing. That is what being unorganized is like. The result of lack of organization is confusion.

Organization does not originate with things you do, but rather, with the kind of person you are. However, by *learning* how to organize outwardly, you can effect changes in *who* you are.

Remember that organization cannot take the place of the right attitudes, the good motivations, or the setting of visions and goals: organization simply helps you walk efficiently along the path and in the direction those other things have set for you.

E. B. Osborn, president of Economics Laboratory, Inc. of New York, has said:[6]

"If your aim is control, it must be self-control first. If your aim is management, it must be self-management first. Beside the task of acquiring the ability to organize a day's work, all else you will ever learn about management is but child's play."

☆ ☆

Order is heaven's first law.[7]
— Alexander Pope

☆ ☆

If you are not naturally an organized person, there are a number of excellent books and resources to help you:

- The Daytimer System of Allentown, Pennsylvania.[8]

This system involves calendars, planners, and diaries.

- Books I can recommend include Alan Lakein's *How to Get Control of Your Time and Your Life*,[9] which outlines a complete, usable organizational system; Stephanie Winston's *The Organized Executive*;[10] Michael LeBoeuf's *Working Smart*;[11] and Alex MacKenzie's *The Time Trap*, which we have already mentioned.

Misconceptions About Organization

In *The Organized Executive*, Ms. Winston lists a number of common assumptions about organizing — none of which are true. Paraphrased into my own style and field, they are:

- Order is not synonymous with neatness.

- Disorganization indicates weakness and lack of moral fiber.

- Creative people are sloppy and disorganized.

- You were born a disorganized person.

- Organization requires an inflexible regimen.

- Organization is bureaucratic, related to nitpicking, and beneath the actions of people who are capable of thinking great thoughts and having great ideas.

• Your secretary should be able to organize you.

None of these are true!

Instead, these are the facts:

• Disorganization is neither your fate nor in your genes. The ability to make sense of random data is a fundamental human attribute.

• Guilt over being disorganized is inappropriate *unless* you already know it comes from laziness or from rebellion against authority. Then guilt should lead to repentance and to change.

• Being organized is not bondage, but really freedom from confusion and chaos.

• "Organizing is, quite simply, a learned skill — a set of methods and tools with which to arrange your time and workload to meet your goals."[12]

☆ ☆

Order is the sanity of the mind,
the health of the body,
the peace of the city
the security of the state.

113

> — *As the beams to a house,*
>   *as the bones to the body,*
>   *so is order to all things.* [13]
>   — Robert Southey

☆ ☆

The Basics of Getting Organized[14]

1. *Set priorities.*

As Beveridge and Davidson pointed out, the first step in getting organized is setting your priorities, deciding what needs to be done first, or what is most important.

Also, this is not a one-time task. Setting priorities is a continuous, every-day process.

2. *Develop a plan.*

Whether it is a long-range goal or a day's work, plan how to get there or to get the things done that need doing — then *stick to your plan*, barring unforeseen circumstances that have to be dealt with.

In that case, deal with the emergency or interruption as quickly as possible, then get back to your plan.

3. *Do not attempt to do everything at once.*

Take one thing at a time — one minute at a time, one hour at a time, one day at a time.

Letting yourself be overwhelmed with an entire project will trigger your body's alarm system. The result will be stress and possibly burnout and/or physical problems.

Develop a system for filing things to work on later.

Make secondary lists.

See what can be given to someone else to do, or what can be eliminated completely as not absolutely necessary.

4. *Make sure you have the tools you need.*

If you need a typewriter, computer, filing cabinets, a desk, storage space, and so forth, arrange to get those things in order of priority.

5. *Organize your work space.*

Your work space should be adequate and comfortable, at least.

It should have proper seating — a good, comfortable chair with back support; ventilation — without adequate oxygen, you get sleepy, and lighting — eyestrain causes headaches at first and eye problems later.

6. *Organize your desk.*

If you are re-organizing your desk, better set aside a certain amount of time to deal with this; if you are arranging a new desk, the task is easier.

    a. Throw away everything that is no longer of any use. Ask yourself these questions:

        "What is the worst thing that can happen if I throw this away?"

        "When is the last time I used it?"

    b. Periodically review your files, keeping only the current, essential ones in your desk. More than 90 percent of all files more than a year old are never used again.

    c. Get trays for "input" and "output."

    d. Once you have your desk organized, keep only the thing you are working on in sight.

    e. Keep items off your desk until you are ready for them. Otherwise, you may be distracted from the main project by something more fun or something that can be done easier. That will throw off your priorities and create snowballing problems as the time goes on.

f. Keep a pad or notebook handy in which to jot down ideas as they come to you. Writing down ideas not only ensures that you will remember them but helps clarify them to your mind.

g. Do not do anything at your desk that is not work. Do not let it become a place to socialize. If you develop the habit of working in a certain place, you will find yourself getting down to business much more rapidly when it is time to work.

Procrastination: the Thief of Time

Procrastination is a deadly pitfall.

There are a number of reasons for putting things off — sometimes it is improper, unrealistic goals, sometimes it is insufficient information, sometimes it is simply not setting a time to complete something.

Goals without deadlines never get reached, or get reached after much delay.

Sometimes procrastination is a result of overcommitment, attempting to do more than is possible. Overcommitment invariably culminates in procrastination.

Another cause of putting things off is unrealistic time elements. Everything takes longer than you expect usually, so you need to allow extra time in estimating any project.

In psychological terms, procrastination is a strategy used to protect people from the basic fears: fear of failure, fear of success, fear of losing a battle, fear of separation, fear of attachment.

☆☆☆☆☆☆☆☆☆☆☆☆☆☆☆☆☆☆☆☆☆☆☆☆

Procrastination allows people to take comfort in believing that their ability is greater than their performance indicates. Perhaps even maintaining the belief that they are brilliant or unlimited in their potential to do well. As long as you procrastinate, you never have to confront the real limits of your ability, whatever those limits are. [15]

☆☆☆☆☆☆☆☆☆☆☆☆☆☆☆☆☆☆☆☆☆☆☆☆

Many times the perfectionist tends toward procrastination. Perfectionism rises not so much in a topnotch perfect behavior as it does in unrealistic attitudes.

The champion athlete, the extremely successful business person, the Nobel prize winner usually knows there will be times of making mistakes, times of having a "bad day," times when his performance will suffer a temporary setback.

They strive for high goals, but are able to tolerate the frustrations and disappointments of sometimes failing to meet those goals. They know they can improve and work hard to do so.

High standards are intended to motivate people toward accomplishment. With perfectionists, those goals often become impossible standards that hinder their efforts — therefore, procrastination results.

If you are going to turn your life around, there will come a time when you must deal with procrastination.

How to Deal With Procrastination

1. Examine your standards to see if they are too high for you to make progress. It is not how high you set your goals that makes you a perfectionist, it is how unrealistic and inhibiting to progress they are for you.

2. Take time to get organized.

When I was in sales, frequently I took time on weekends to organize my car, my clothes, my tools, and my briefcase. That included cleaning the car, inside and out; making sure any clothes that needed attention got to the cleaners or the tailors for mending; emptying and reorganizing my briefcase; making sure my office was neat and clean; and, in general, trying to create a success environment.

Those may seem like little things, but they help you keep motivated and moving in a positive direction. Also, they make a good impression on other people.

Fear is at the root of all avoidance.

Can you really afford putting off a large, important project until the last minute? Suppose unexpected things come up? Then you would fail.

Procrastination causes worry, anxiety, frustration, and stress — to say nothing of possible material losses, such as finances, other jobs, and so forth.

Train yourself out of the habit of procrastination by giving yourself rewards at certain milestones along the way of completing a project and on final completion.

Avoid escapes. Escapes usually give the impression that you are productive when you really are not being productive.

☆ ☆

By the streets of "by and by,"
one arrives at the house of "never."[16]
— Saavedra M. de Cervantes

☆ ☆

Endnotes

[1] Beveridge, Don and Davidson, Jeffrey P. "How to Get Organized," Marriott's *Portfolio* Fall/Winter 1988, p. 44. Adapted from *The Achievement Challenge: How To Be a 10 in Business* (Homewood: Illinois, Dow Jones-Irwin. Copyright © 1988 by Beveridge and Davidson).

[2] Ibid., pp. 44-46.

[3] Ibid., p. 44, with some re-writing for this book.

[4] Ibid.

[5] *The New Dictionary of Thoughts,* p. 458.

[6] Mackenzie, R. Alec. *The Time Trap* (New York: McGraw-Hill Book Company. Copyright © 1972, AMACOM), p. 61.

[7] *The New Dictionary,* p. 458.

[8] Daytimers Inc., One Day-Timer Plaza, Allentown, Pennsylvania 18195.

[9] Lakein, Alan. *How to Get Control of Your Time and Your Life.* (New York: Wyden, Copyright © 1973).

[10] Winston, Stephanie. *The Organized Executive: New Ways to Manage Time, Paper, and People* (New York: Warner Books. Copyright © 1983 by Stephanie Winston.) Reprinted with permission. An earlier Warner book by Ms. Winston also would be helpful, *Getting Organized: The Easy Way to Put Your Life in Order.*

[11] LeBoeuf, Michael. *Working Smart: How to Accomplish More in Half the Time* (New York: Warner Books. Copyright © 1979 by Michael LeBoeuf).

[12] *The Organized Executive,* p. 21.

[13] *The New Dictionary,* p. 458.

[14] Beveridge and Davidson.

[15] Burka, Jane B. and Yuen, Lenora M. *Procrastination: Why You Do It, What to Do About It.* (Reading, Massachusetts: Addison-Wesley, Copyright © 1983).

[16] *The New Dictionary,* p. 520.

Chapter 9
DO YOU HAVE A MINUTE?

There is a time to be born,
and a time to die, says Solomon,
and it is the memento of a truly wise man;
but there is an interval between these two times
of infinite importance. [1]
— Leigh Richmond

☆☆☆☆☆☆☆☆☆☆☆☆☆☆☆☆☆☆☆☆☆☆☆☆

To waste your time is to waste your life.

To master your time is to master your life.

Being effective in anything means first selecting the best of all available possibilities and doing it the best way.

However, effective businessmen or athletes, in my observations, do not start planning or operating with their tasks — they start with the *time* they have available.

They do not begin with planning; they begin with finding out where their time is presently going.

Then they attempt to manage their time and cut back the unproductive demands.

Finally they consolidate their discretionary time into the largest possible continuing units. To do this, they use a three-step process:

- They record their time;

- They manage their time;

- They consolidate their time.

Systematic time management is critically important.

☆ ☆

Time was is past; thou canst not it recall:
Time is, thou hast; employ the portion small;
Time future is not; and may never be:
Time present is the only time for thee.[2]
— Lydia H. Sigourney

☆ ☆

When all is said and done, time is the most important asset you have, and *control* possibly is the most important key word in dealing with time management.

Control does not mean allowing your schedule to run you, but it does mean enough structure to get things done and still allow you to be flexible and spontaneous.

Perhaps you think outside factors are controlling your life and keeping you from getting things done — when it could be you who are not doing a good job in those areas where you *do* have control.

Your time is a result of hundreds of thousands of big and little choices made each year.

The Ideal Is "Balance"

Too much organization is as ineffective as too little.

When there is an overemphasis on organization, many things are tied up in all kinds of red tape, and it is very hard to get anything accomplished.

The key is to work smarter, not harder.

The biggest payoff is your time, and the life you have when you learn to manage your time will show greater freedom.

Your time is limited, but your imagination is not.

There are a lot of new and creative ways that can be found to manage time.

Managing time means sorting between what *must* be done, what *should* be done, and what *can* be done if there is time left.

Most people in just a few minutes of daydreaming can come up with a lot of activities to keep them busy for weeks and days!

It is easy to think of things — some interesting and others just "busy work" — that sometimes keep you from getting to the essential task.

15 Top Time-Wasters

Experience in fourteen countries with managers at various levels in diverse organizations led to a clear picture of time-wasters that afflict managers generally. In everyone's list, five things ranked at or near the top.[3] They are:

1. Telephone interruptions.

2. Drop-in visitors.

3. Meetings (schedule and unscheduled).

4. Crises.

5. Lack of objectives, priorities, and deadlines.

These five were followed closely by another group of five time thieves:

6. Cluttered desk and personal disorganization.

7. Ineffective delegation and personal involvement in routine affairs and small details.

8. Attempting too much at once, unrealistic time estimates.

9. Confused chains of authority and responsibility.

10. Inadequate, inaccurate, or delayed information.

Depending upon the group, particular leadership styles, and organization characteristics, other time-wasters often included another set of five things:

11. Indecision and procrastination.

12. Lack of, or unclear, communication and instructions.

13. Inability to say "no."

14. Lack of controls, standards, and progress reports to keep track of the completion of tasks.

15. Fatigue and lack of self-discipline.

Many additional time-wasters have been identified, of course, ranging from the harried (looking for lost files) to the humorous (girls in short skirts) to the ridiculous (answering foolish questions) to the dubious (liquid lunches)!

☆ ☆

A man's time, when well-husbanded, is like
a cultivated field,
of which a few acres produces more
of what is useful to life
than extensive provinces,
even of the richest soil
when overrun with weeds and brambles.[4]
— David Hume

☆ ☆

It would be profitable for you to sit down and make your own list to give you a starting point for eliminating personal time-wasters.

Take a typical day, list everything you do — even telephone calls, visits to the bathroom, and time for "breaks" or lunch — then go over the list to see what could have been eliminated. Be ruthless in marking time-wasters.

☆ ☆

*Planning is bringing the future into the present
so that we can do something about it.*

☆ ☆

How do you make decisions about what to do and what not to do?

Most of us make decisions based on these reasons:

- Habit — the way we always have done it.

- Demands of others — "the squeaking hinge gets the oil."

- Escapism, or the desire to retreat.

- Spur of the moment — impulse.

- By default — not making a decision *not* to.

- Conscious decision — the motivation that ought to be at the top of the list is on the bottom.

A good planner keeps checking as the day goes by, or the week, or the month to see if his plans are being followed and his priorities are being carried out.

It is important to keep this checklist on yourself because:

- *You cannot manage what you do not measure.*

- People who do not keep records do not make records.

Look for problems, false assumptions, hangups, and other difficulties — then make corrections where necessary.

Many people have trouble planning, because they consider it just *thinking,* and wind up staring off into space and daydreaming.

☆☆☆☆☆☆☆☆☆☆☆☆☆☆☆☆☆☆☆☆☆☆☆

Time is what we want most,
but what, alas! we use worst. [5]

— William Penn

☆☆☆☆☆☆☆☆☆☆☆☆☆☆☆☆☆☆☆☆☆☆☆

Do First Things First

In all planning — whether it is visions and goals or time management — you need to do two things:

- Make a list,

- Set priorities.

Charles Schwab paid Ivy Lee $25,000 for the formula of organizing that follows. [6] It seems deceptively simply, but is enormously helpful.

Ivy Lee Formula

1. List the six most important things for tomorrow.

2. Give them a number in order of priority.

3. Tackle one at a time and stick with it until you complete it.

4. Spend the last minutes of the day listing the six most important items for tomorrow.

This enables you to *do first things first*.

Writing down goals in order of priorities, even on a day-by-day basis, is important. It is particularly important to write down lifetime goals.

Unwritten goals often remain vague or utopian dreams, such as travel or becoming a millionaire.

Writing down goals tends to make them more concrete and specific and helps you probe beneath the surface of some cliches you have been telling yourself for years.

Many times, we are lying to ourselves or making excuses for not getting certain things done.

☆ ☆

I often tell my son:
"If 'ifs' and 'buts' were candy and nuts —
we'd all have a merry Christmas!"

☆ ☆

Every Friday afternoon, you can review the whole week just past and lay out the next week's schedule.

Tips for Making Schedules

In laying out a weekly schedule, the key is to block out time for top-priority jobs:

• Reserve a particular day of the week — say Tuesday or Tuesday morning — for major projects.

• Even if your schedule is broken up with interruptions, you can attempt to keep certain blocks of time intact for high-value priorities.

Remember: *there is always enough time for the important things.*

• Trying to do the same thing at the same time each day conserves and generates energy.

You have two kinds of "prime time":

• *Internal prime time* is the time when you know you work the best, whether it is morning or afternoon.

• *External prime time* is the best time to attend to other people, those you must deal with either on the job, socially, or at home.

Try to save external time for prime projects.

• Build flexibility into your schedule.

1. Reserve an hour a day that is uncommitted.

2. Leave holes for interviews, conversations, or whatever else that may run longer than scheduled.

3. Set aside time to read the mail and catch up on paperwork.

• Do not neglect your personal life. Build in time for this as well.

Many men who make their personal lives subordinate to their careers fail in the end. I have seen this with athletes who are great leaders on the sports fields, but who fail to lead in any areas of their home lives.

This is frustrating to their wives, causes bitterness, and shortchanges their children. In other words, it is unfair to your wife and children when they are not included in your priorities.

• Do not put in too many hours of overtime.

The more overtime a person puts in, the more exhausted he is, and the less efficient he becomes. The answer is not to spend more time on a project, but to work more effectively in the time allotted.

You cannot work as effectively if you are fatigued from excessive hours.

☆ ☆

When it is built into your schedule properly,
doing nothing is not a waste of time.

☆ ☆

• Schedule time to relax among your priorities.

If you arrange things so that you have time to relax and do nothing, you will not only get more done but have more fun doing it!

When I first started in the life insurance business, I was excited about the fact that I could work seven days a week as many hours as I wished.

However, as I began to cut my selling time to five days and then to four, I found I was able to do more business than when I had the whole week stretched out in front of me to see people any time of the day or evening.

• Use the time you do have more wisely.

Why spend two hours at lunch, when back in the office, the phones are quiet and other people are gone?

Eat quickly and lightly — which also will keep you from getting sleepy or tired in the afternoon — and use that time to get things done that need concentration.

If you are a homemaker, use the time when the children are at school or taking naps.

If you are an employer, allow your people to read, write, or whatever after their scheduled work is done.

You cannot push people to be creative by the clock. Beyond a certain point, simply putting in hours is not the best way to get creative work done.

Unless you schedule time for relaxation or creativity, you will not have it.

If you allow it, there will always be enough work to spill over into any free time.

✰✰✰✰✰✰✰✰✰✰✰✰✰✰✰✰✰✰✰✰✰✰✰✰

Work does expand to fill the time available.

— Parkinson's Law

✰✰✰✰✰✰✰✰✰✰✰✰✰✰✰✰✰✰✰✰✰✰✰✰

In addition to scheduling enough periods of relaxation during the week, it pays in the long run to take a look two or three months ahead, see what is planned, and set the time aside on a monthly or a quarterly basis to take an extended period of time off. Perhaps it is just a long weekend, but it will pay off in increased efficiency over the long run.

Evaluating Lifetime Goals, or Use of Time

As I mentioned earlier, insurance statistics show the mortality rate is running 100 percent!

Occasionally — perhaps once a year on your birthday — it is a good idea to take a look at any progress you have made toward your long-range goals. This will give you an opportunity to re-evaluate, make changes, or tighten up your time schedule.

Areas that affect a lifetime, not just the immediate days or weeks, are sleeping and eating.

People in the medical profession have found that many of us spend more hours in sleep than we really need. We do it out of:

- Habit,

- Escape,

- Depression.

Find out by experimenting exactly how much sleep you need to feel at your best, then stick to that number of hours.

How you eat is as important as the kinds of food that you eat — the slower you eat, the less you eat, and the better it is digested. Usually, it takes about twenty minutes for your stomach to feel full. Most of us eat too fast, not allowing time for our systems to register what is being taken in, and then we eat too much and feel sluggish for a couple of hours.

If you eat a light lunch slowly while you are unwinding, you will feel better after a twenty-minute lunch at your desk than if you rush out, fight the lunch-rush crowds, hastily swallow more food than you need, and rush back to work.

☆ ☆

The Golden Rule of Time Management:
Make a special effort to be considerate
of other people's time,
And they will be likely to respect your time.

☆ ☆

"Do you have a minute?" usually means, "May I have your attention now to talk about something that will take an unspecified amount of time?"

When someone asks you for a minute, you need to learn to say, "If it *really* is just a minute, yes. But if this is going to take longer, let's plan our talk for later."

During my years with The Northwestern Mutual Insurance Company, they were called "the quiet company" because they did very little advertising. The firm carried that concept farther and regularly scheduled "quiet days," when calls from agents were fielded and messages taken. Employees in the home office would have those days to work without interruptions. That time-management idea was very productive.

☆☆☆☆☆☆☆☆☆☆☆☆☆☆☆☆☆☆☆☆☆☆☆☆

The Swiss-cheese method of accomplishing tasks is to take a project and poke holes in it a little at a time, but stay with it until it is done. [7]

☆☆☆☆☆☆☆☆☆☆☆☆☆☆☆☆☆☆☆☆☆☆☆☆

There are seven common mistakes, seven critical ways of escape, that take you away from high priorities:

Indulging yourself, socializing, reading, doing things yourself that could be delegated, overdoing, running away, and daydreaming "how to do better next time."

The cliche, "Where there's a will, there's a way," is *true*.

Stick to your time schedule.

Be determined.

Set your will.

Do not push yourself beyond endurance, however.

Increase willpower by practicing in easy situations.

Make your priorities exciting.

Slow down making final decisions as long as you can so that you have time to make conscious, deliberate choices.

Do not let your emotions make your decisions.

Do not waste time worrying about what went wrong.

☆ ☆

*Most people spend their lives
minimizing losses rather than maximizing gains.*

☆ ☆

Endnotes

[1] *The New Dictionary,* p. 672.

[2] Ibid., p. 675.

[3] Mackenzie, R. Alec. Adapted from "Troubleshooting Chart for Time-Wasters," *Managing Time at the Top* (New York: The President's Association, 1970).

[4] *The New Dictionary,* p. 675

[5] Ibid.

[6] Ivy Lee Formula.

[7] Lakein. *How to Get Control of Your Time and Your Life,* p. 49.

Chapter 10

YOU CAN'T TAKE IT WITH YOU, BUT IT SURE COMES IN HANDY NOW

*If your outgo exceeds your income
your upkeep will be your downfall.*

✩✩✩✩✩✩✩✩✩✩✩✩✩✩✩✩✩✩✩✩✩✩✩✩✩

When we speak of staying in the game to get to a turning point, there probably is no area in a person's life that has a greater need for a turning point than *finances*!

Because of the "buy now-pay later" philosophy that took root in this country shortly after the Great Depression, many of us live way over our income.

☆ ☆

Winners are not people without any problems.
Winners are people who have learned how to overcome
their problems. [1]

— Mike Murdock

☆ ☆

When I was in the insurance industry, occasionally people would encourage me to go out and buy something I could not afford in order to give me the motivation to work hard to pay for it!

That worked for a period of time, and will work for you for a period of time — until the storms of life hit. Then it will be shown up as a destructive policy by which to live.

In my life, the "storm" was divorce and subsequent depression.

We had lived in a high level of indebtedness, which I was able to service and keep paid as long as I worked steadily.

However, as depression set in — after having to move out of my house and see my children on visits rather than being their full-time father — I became despondent.

When I became despondent, I began not to call on clients or not to complete sales on the contacts I did make.

Very quickly, banks and credit card companies began to make calls on me! They wanted their bills paid.

True, I was depressed, but some of what was going on was being slothful, simply not being diligent.

I spent a lot of time sleeping as an escape.

One thing led to another, and I came to the point where my finances were destroyed completely. From having a sterling credit rating, suddenly I had none. Before my divorce, I could pick up the phone, borrow $5,000, and pick up the money at the end of the day.

Even today, almost ten years later, I am still — in a sense — in the process of restoring finances.

☆ ☆

One of the major concerns in America today is our national debt, which is simply an extension of the philosophy by which we have learned to run our personal lives.

The world's system of finances seems to be failing. Certainly, we can see that it is not working productively or efficiently!

Americans seem to have restless spirits and a sense of disillusionment with present conditions.

☆☆☆☆☆☆☆☆☆☆☆☆☆☆☆☆☆☆☆☆☆☆☆☆

A small fire can easily be put out with a little water, but if the fire is raging uncontrollably, it is best to contain it. . .to create boundaries. . .and then, in effect, to say to the fire:

"Burn all you want inside of the circle, but you may not cross the line!"

☆☆☆☆☆☆☆☆☆☆☆☆☆☆☆☆☆☆☆☆☆☆☆☆

Perhaps it is time to create boundaries on personal debt as well as on the national debt.

Some Steps for Overcoming Financial Adversity[2]

1. Recognize and name the adversity for what it is. Face your financial problems. You must confront before you can correct.

2. See your problem as a project. Look at the problem as an opportunity for victory. Make the crisis a challenge. It is not fatal — usually. It is not "the end."

3. Identify the reasons for this financial crisis.

4. Create alternative spending patterns.

5. Re-evaluate your spending habits.

6. Inform and involve others in your project of overhauling your financial pattern.

   a. Challenge your family.

   b. Use financial consultants, also books.

   c. Share your situation with creditors. Usually, if a creditor knows you are being honest with him and are trying to meet your obligation, he will work with you.

7. Consider alternative or additional income possibilities.

   a. It may be time to change jobs or careers.

   b. It may be time to seek a promotion.

   c. It may be time to consider a new investment.

Disconnect from comfort or convenience; be creative.

One of President Jimmy Carter's more successful speeches contained much truth: He pointed out that our attitudes toward money can become a "religion" that is contradictory to the principles of Christianity.

☆ ☆

In a nation that was proud of hard work, strong families, close-knit communities and our faith in God, too many of us now tend to worship self-indulgence and consumption. Human identity is no longer defined by what one does, but by what one owns. But we have discovered that owning things and consuming things does not satisfy our longing for meaning. We have learned that piling up material goods cannot fill the emptiness of lives which have no confidence or purpose. [3]

☆ ☆

Ownership or Stewardship

A classic in the area of finances and Christianity is Larry Burkett's *Your Finances in Changing Times.*

This book, with a foreword by Dr. Billy Graham, was first published in 1975. In it, Burkett wrote:

> Most individual tension, family friction, strife, anger, and frustration are caused directly or indirectly by money. But for the Christian seeking God's best, He has established basic principles for the management of possessions. [4]

Here are some of those principles, as found in Burkett's book:

1. We were made stewards over the earth's resources (Gen. 1:28). Each of us is a manager, *not an owner*. God is the owner, and we are to manage according to *His* plan.

2. *You can't take it with you!*
   The only thing you "take with you" is what you did with what was entrusted to you.

☆ ☆

Someone asked John D. Rockefeller's chief accountant how much the immensely wealthy man left.

The accountant answered, "Everything!"

☆ ☆

3. God expects those with the ability to invest to do so, but He also expects a return on what He has given you. (The Parable of the Talents — Matt. 25:14-30. "Talents" in Bible days were money. The parable is teaching about proper use of money.)

4. God will never use money in a Christian's life to worry him, corrupt him, build his ego, or to satisfy self-indulgence.

5. Hoarding money is not a godly principle.

6. There is nothing *inherently* spiritual in poverty, nor is there sin in wealth — only in the *love* of wealth or possessions. (1 Tim. 6:10.)

7. God's laws are no respecter of persons.

8. God has promised to meet our needs, as long as we put Him first.

9. God's laws on finances are as fixed as His laws in physics. His principle of sowing and reaping (Matt. 13) works for anyone — "the rain shines on the just and the unjust alike" (Matt. 5:45) — just as His law of gravity works for saint as well as sinner.

What Is Prosperity?

The world approaches *prosperity* on a one-dimensional basis.

God teaches *prosperity* on a multi-dimensional basis: spirit, soul, and body:

a) Second Corinthians 5:17 says the spirit of man is made new through salvation (accepting Jesus as Savior).

b) Psalm 23 says the Lord "restores" the soul.

c) Isaiah 53:4,5 says the body is healed from sickness and disease.

In the Kingdom of God, *prosperity* is founded first on a relationship as son or daughter, then on an intimate friendship with God, initiated and maintained through prayer and studying His Word.

☆ ☆

Seek ye first the kingdom of God,
and his righteousness;
and all these things shall be added unto you.
— Matthew 6:33

☆ ☆

Prosperity in God's economy comes when you want to praise and worship Him rather than deify self through self-indulgence in consuming this world's goods.

Prosperity in God's economy is described as *giving*, not getting.

Prosperity in God's economy is not based on class, race, gender, or nationality — only on the attitude of the heart.

Millions of Americans may have money and possessions, but they are not prosperous as God defines prosperity.

They are not leading fulfilled and successful lives in terms of basic values.

The world measures *prosperity* by the profit and loss statement, good looks, appearances, rank in the community. People using this standard look on relationships as a means to an end. An individual's value is measured by his usefulness to them.

Most of the time, people who base their lifestyles and attitudes on these values end up empty, weak, insecure, and fearful — in other words, very unprosperous.

The Flip Side of Lust for Money

If the world goes to the extreme in making wealth an idol. . .if some Christians have gone to the extreme in applying God's principles strictly to financial prosperity. . .*more* Christians have distorted the principles of the Kingdom and made an idol of poverty.

The attitude toward money that prevails in the majority of the Church today is a throw-back to medieval society.

Jeremy Rifkin says that making money in medieval times was not a sign of accomplishment but of antisocial behavior.[5]

Then, church leaders believed merchandising and the accumulation of the goods of this world (by individuals) focused attention on *this* life instead of the next one. People would put out just the amount of energy necessary to provide for their bodily needs. Then they quit, unless they were serfs (close to slavery).

Laws were made and carried out through the church of those days that hindered the chances of most people to gain individual wealth.

The Reformation began to overturn a thousand years of thinking that "poor is better," and "poverty is next to godliness." Theologian John Calvin was primarily responsible. In the mid-1500s, Calvin became the father of the modern "work ethic." Rifkin writes:[6]

> Maximum output, contended Calvin, was as important as maximum input....Since the surplus was never intended for the benefit of the individual but only to serve the glory of God, it would be sinful to lavish it on one's carnal appetites. On the other hand, *there was nothing sinful about the surplus itself.* ...
>
> ...the idea that the product of one's labor was designed to serve God's glory and not people's appetites fit neatly with later capitalist theories that saw labor as merely one of several purely utilitarian factors in the production process. Instead of people serving God, however, they began to serve the capitalists instead...(which was not Calvin's intention at all).

In the world and in Christianity, we still see both extremes:

> *Wealth and possessions are the ultimate*
> *desired end in life;*
> *Wealth is sin.*

Both premises are false.

☆ ☆

> *Money is a training ground*
> *for God to develop (and for us to discover)*
> *our trustworthiness.* [7]

☆ ☆

God's *war on poverty* involves putting wealth and possessions in the proper perspective to Him.

Some Secrets to Abundance

1. A crisis is a signal for me to learn, not lose.

2. It is not a sin to have a need in my life. On the other hand, my need is an indication to change something in my life.

3. There is always a reason for my lack. Six Bible reasons for poverty are:

   • an unteachable spirit.............Prov. 13:18

- laziness .... Prov. 24:33,34

- ignorance .... Prov. 24:4, Hosea 4:6

- oppressing the poor .... Prov. 22:16,22

- misfortune .... 1 Kings 17

- withholding .... Prov. 11:24-26

4. God will vary His methods of supply.

5. Sometimes God will remove my visible sources of supply to maintain my dependency upon Him.

6. He sometimes uses the illogical and the unlikely to supply my needs.

7. God will not ask me for something I do not have. God will ask me for something I hang onto.

8. My supply for tomorrow can start with whatever I have in my hand today: God's laws of sowing and reaping. (Gen. 1:11,12,21,24,25; Gal. 6:7.) Everyone has something to give.[8]

☆ ☆

The world gives to get; Christians get to give.

☆ ☆

9. Circumstances do not control a Christian's supply. My expectations and my words affect my supply.

10. When I let go of what is in my hand, God will let go of what is in His hand.

☆☆☆☆☆☆☆☆☆☆☆☆☆☆☆☆☆☆☆☆☆☆☆☆

God does not supply money to satisfy our every whim and desire. His promise is to meet our needs and provide an abundance so that we can help other people.

It is when we accept this principle that God will multiply our abundance as well. [9]

— Larry Burkett

☆☆☆☆☆☆☆☆☆☆☆☆☆☆☆☆☆☆☆☆☆☆☆

How To Manage Your Money

1. First of all, *couples need to agree* on certain goals, certain needs, and philosophies of spending.

This requires communication.

Example: The husband may have grown up in a family that took care of immediate needs — such as food or clothes, and so forth — first and paid bills with what is left. If the wife has learned that one pays bills first and does without immediate needs if necessary, then there is a built-in conflict on spending.

More than likely, the first thing that happens is that each will defend his "learned" attitude and attack the other's. Money is one of the primary areas of marital problems.

The only way to get around this is to examine what you believe to see if it is valid, then come to a compromise with the other — or totally throw out your premise, if you see it is not valid in your situation or not worth the strife and contention it brings.

☆ ☆

*Information without application
leads to frustration.* [10]
— Larry Burkett

☆ ☆

2. *Make a Budget.*

(If you are a single head of household, or self-employed, or head of a business, this is your first step.)

155

Why is a budget necessary?

a) To find out where the money is going.

b) To control where the money will go.

c) To set priorities in spending.

"The initial tendency is to create an unrealistic budget....The next tendency is to create a budget — and then stop!...There is no magic in a budget; it is only a written expression of what you must do to be a good steward."[11]

3. *You really need two budgets.*

    A. The first determines your present status.

    B. The second determines your goals.

4. *Where to begin?*

    Step 1. List expenses on a monthly basis, both fixed and variable.

    Step 2. List available income per month.

    Step 3. Compare income versus expenses.

If your income exceeds your outgo, then you only need to establish budget control.

If expenses exceed income, additional steps are necessary.

5. *Analyze Your Expenditures.*

Steps 1, 2, and 3 are: **Keep records!**

a) Balance your bank accounts carefully.

b) Allow for hidden expenditures, such as books, magazines, eating out, cosmetics, impulse buying, gifts.

6. *Hints to Reduce Impulse Spending.*

a) Make a practice of giving yourself a "cooling off" period before making the actual purchase.

b) Make a habit of comparison shopping.

c) *Never* use credit cards for impulse buying.

d) Cut down on "window shopping" or "cruising the malls."

In my personal life, one of the most exciting things I have done was get God involved in my finances.

Paul Pruyser wrote:

Religions have advocated time and again the idea of stewardship in order to regulate man's attitude toward things, especially possessions.[12]

I would challenge those reading this book to make a decision to get God involved in their finances.

☆ ☆

You cannot borrow your way out of debt,
*but you can **give** your way out.*

☆ ☆

If I could capsulize my advice, it would be:

Keep good records, be diligent in your work, get God involved by tithing and giving — "planting seeds" — and study the Bible to see that God will keep His promises. Therefore, He *will* provide a harvest.

What you sow, you shall certainly reap in finances as well as in anything else. Begin to give to others, not just with finances, but in service, in love, in help of other kinds.

Endnotes

[1]Murdock, Mike. "10 Steps for Overcoming Financial Adversity," Mike Murdock Achievement Seminar, P. O. Box 47550, Dallas, Texas 75247, Wisdom Study Guide 501, p. 1.

[2]Ibid., pp. 1-3.

[3]Greider, William. *Secrets of the Temple, How the Federal Reserve Runs the Country* (New York: Simon & Schuster, Inc. Copyright © 1987 by William Greider), p. 14.

[4]Burkett, Larry. *Your Finances in Changing Times* (Chicago: Moody Press, Revised Edition 1982. Copyright © 1975 by Christian Financial Concepts), p. 39. Principles adapted from Chapter 4.

[5]Rifkin, Jeremy with Howard, Ted. *The Emerging Order, God in the Age of Scarcity* (New York: G. P. Putnam's Sons. Copyright © 1979 by Jeremy Rifkin with Ted Howard).

[6]Ibid., p. 21.

[7]Burkett, *Your Finances,* p. 43.

[8]Adapted from "25 Secrets to Abundance," Wisdom Study Guide 502 by Mike Murdock, Dallas, Texas 75247.

[9]Burkett, p. 53.

[10]Ibid.

[11]Burkett, p. 149. The budget section is adapted in part from Burkett's *Your Finances in Changing Times,* Chapter 14.

[12]Pruyser, Paul. *A Dynamic Psychology of Religion.* (New York: Harper & Row, Inc. 1968.)

Chapter 11
VISIT YOUR
"ADULT" BOOKSTORE

I was in a Christian bookstore one day when a man walked in, and after looking around a few minutes, he asked, "Where are the adult books?"

Obviously, he was looking for the popular magazines that display nude women, but the proprietor enthusiastically answered, "Sir, all we carry in here are adult books!"

☆ ☆

I urge you to visit your "adult" bookstore.

In 1968, I attended a seminar held by Charles Jones, president of Life Management Services of Harrisburg, Pennsylvania. One of the great thoughts he shared then is that you will be the same five years from now as you are today — except for two things:

- The people you meet.

- The books you read.

I have found that to be true.

Readers are not all leaders; however, nearly all leaders are readers.

No one is too young to begin learning that everyone is a leader: You lead to or away from things.

The type of person you are going to be five years from now is being determined right now. If you want your life to be productive and positive, you need to learn the difference between *investing* your time and *spending* your time.

Through books, you can have a dialogue with the great people, the leaders, of all ages — those who were winners.

I am going to talk about some life-changing books that you can use to help turn your life around.

☆☆☆☆☆☆☆☆☆☆☆☆☆☆☆☆☆☆☆☆☆☆☆

In the best books, great men talk to us,
give us their most precious thoughts,
and pour their souls into ours. [1]
— Channing

☆☆☆☆☆☆☆☆☆☆☆☆☆☆☆☆☆☆☆☆☆☆☆

Book One: The Bible

The book at the top of the list is, of course, the Bible. It is absolutely amazing when we begin to be doers of the Word, and not hearers only, what begins to take place in our lives.

For a Christian, the Bible is a long letter from the Father.

However, even for a non-Christian, the Bible is worth reading. Until after World War II, a person was not considered well-educated unless he at least was familiar with the Bible.

Sayings from the Word still are sprinkled through our language, but many people do not know the origins of the expressions they use. Many best-sellers in the past, and even today, have titles that are phrases right out of the Bible.

What Some People Have Said About the Bible

The morality of the Bible is, after all, the safety of society. [2]
(F. C. Monfort)

The Bible, thoroughly known, is literature in itself. . . . [3]
(James Anthony Froude)

We account the Scriptures of God to be the most sublime philosophy. I find more sure marks of authenticity in the

163

Bible than in any profane history whatever. [4] (Isaac Newton)

The Holy Bible is not only great but high explosive literature. [5] (Stanley Baldwin)

All the distinctive features and superiority of our republican institutions are derived from the teachings of Scripture. [6] (Edward Everett)

No lawyer can afford to be ignorant of the Bible. [7] (Rufus Choate)

Every great book that has been published since the first printing press was invented has directly or indirectly derived much of its power from the Sacred Oracles. [8] (DeWitt Talmadge, Herald of Holiness)

- **George Washington:** "It is impossible to rightly govern the world without God and the Bible."

- **Charles Dickens:** "The New Testament is the very best book that ever was or ever will be known in the world."

- **Andrew Jackson:** "That book, sir, is the rock on which our republic rests."

- **Horace Greeley:** "It is impossible to mentally or socially enslave a Bible-reading people. The principles of the Bible are the groundwork of human freedom."

• **Warning:** This book (the Bible) is habit-forming. Regular use causes loss of anxiety, decreased appetite for lying, cheating, stealing, hating. Symptoms: increased sensations of love, peace, joy, compassion.[9]

For a number of years, I owned a Bible without realizing that it was full of wisdom and principles for everyday life, much less that it literally was the Word of God.

Joshua 1:8 says that when we keep the Word in our mouths, when we meditate it, when we observe it, when we do it — then we make our ways prosperous and have good success.

Milestones in My Path

I can look back at the points in my path where someone came along and introduced me to each of the following books, and each book brought revelation and changed me in some way. There are twelve books, one for each month of the year.

1. *My Utmost for His Highest* by Oswald Chambers.[10]

Daily devotions designed to lift your sights and let your spirits soar. A classic in encouragement to the human spirit.

2. *Could You Not Tarry One Hour?* by Dr. Larry Lea.[11]

Dr. Lea, pastor of Church on the Rock, Rockwall, Texas, presents his experience in a teaching on personal prayer. He shows how to find joy in spending a long daily period in prayer. Through this book you will discover a way of entering the Lord's presence that will change your life. You will learn how to move from feeling prayer is drudgery to delighting in it.

3. *Life Is Tremendous,* by Charles "T." Jones.[12]

"Tremendous" Jones' book, a classic in the field of Christian motivational literature, shows how you can be happy, involved, relevant, productive, healthy, and secure in the midst of a high-pressure, commercialized, automated, pill-prone society.

It is not easy nor automatic — but it is possible through the development of certain personal qualities that make up the traits of leadership.

You can be a leader, because *leaders are made, not born.*

4. *How I Raised Myself From Failure to Success in Selling* by Frank Bettger.[13]

Universally appealing, Bettger's book holds an *idea* that lies at the very heart of outstanding success in life. Also, this book puts in your hands a *method* for implementing that idea every waking minute of every day.

Taken together, this *idea* and this *method* create the long-sought formula for achievement that can be used by anyone, a formula that always works and can be applied to any desired goal. It literally puts any constructive goal well within your reach.

5. *Psycho-Cybernetics* by Maxwell Maltz.[14]

This is a how-to book that prepares the individual to be successful. Success has nothing to do with prestige symbols, but with creative accomplishment. Rightly speaking, no man should attempt to be "a success," but everyone can and should attempt to be "successful."

6. *Maximized Manhood* by Edwin Louis Cole.[15]

Written specifically for men, this book is not merely a rhetorical discussion of things that are crucial in the lives of men, but is a head-on confrontation with those issues.

It brings into modern life a type of writing that has been sadly deficient for many years — "man-to-man" talks on virtues, real manhood, sex, and a respect for women and children. In other words, this book discusses the meaning of being "a grown man."

7. *Man's Search for Meaning* by Dr. Victor E. Frankl.[16]

After three grim years at Auschwitz and other Nazi prisons, Dr. Frankl gained his freedom only to learn that almost all of his entire family had been wiped out. However, during — or partly because of — the almost incredible suffering and degradations of those harrowing years, he developed his theory of *logotherapy,* a theory that makes the concept of man into a whole and focuses attention upon mankind's groping for a higher meaning in life.

8. *The Making of a Champion* by Dr. Lester Sumrall.[17]

Dr. Sumrall has found in the Old Testament hero, Nehemiah, the true traits of a champion. In this book, you are "walked" through the book of Nehemiah and shown how integrity, prayer, faithfulness, compassion, humility, initiative, and "a holy stubbornness" can be developed and used to accomplish God's plans for you.

Just as Nehemiah rebuilt the walls of Jerusalem from the rubble of the old, you can turn old habits and excuses into traits that will make you a winning, victorious "overcomer" in life.

9. *The Tongue — A Creative Force* by Charles Capps.[18]

Words are the most powerful things in the universe. The words you speak will either put you over in life or hold you in bondage. Many people are held prisoner by their circumstances because of their words. The absence of positive words in your life will rob you of the faith necessary to release ability.

10. *How Faith Works* by Dr. Frederick K.C. Price.[19]

This book is the primer for every believer who desires to step beyond the natural circumstances of life into the supernatural flow of God.

11. *Truths That Transform* by D. James Kennedy.[20]

This book is for those who have yearned for a deeper understanding of Christian truth and what it can mean in their lives. It is designed to open your eyes to the spiritual potential in everyday life through a deeper knowledge of the teaching of the Scriptures.

12. *Prayers That Avail Much* by Germaine Copeland.[21]

One of the best sellers in the Christian field, this book developed out of a group of intercessors who began to search the Bible for answers to problems about which they were praying.

Prayer is not a formality, but is the "living" Word in your mouth. This is a collection of prayers based on Scripture that you can use to begin talking to the Lord about *any* problem in your life.

For Other Reading and Listening

Books

1. Allen, James. *As a Man Thinketh*, Peter Pauper Press.

2. Ash, Mary Kay. *On People Management*, Warner Books, 1984.

3. Carnegie, Dale. *How to Win Friends and Influence People*, Pocket Books, 1982.

4. Gordon, Maynard M. *The Iacocca Management Technique*, Ballantine Books, 1985.

5. Murdock, Mike. *Wisdom for Winning*, Harrison House, 1988.

6. Rodgers, Buck. *The IBM Way,* Harper & Row, 1986.

7. Schwartz, David J. *The Magic of Thinking Big,* Simon & Schuster, 1983.

Tapes

1. "The Price of Leadership," Charles "T." Jones.

2. "Lead the Field," Earl Nightingale.

3. "Success and the Self Image," Zig Ziglar.

4. "How Faith Works," Frederick K. C. Price.

5. "The Secrets of Power Negotiating," Roger Dawson.

6. "The Psychology of Achievement," Brian Tracy.

7. "See You at the Top," Zig Ziglar.

8. "Seeds of Greatness," Denis Waitley.

9. "How To Win," Jerry Savelle.

10. "Your Time and Your Life," Charles R. Hobbs.

11. "What They Don't Teach You at Harvard Business School," Mark H. McCormack.

12. "The Executive Treasury of Humor, Vol. I-VI," Nightingale-Conant.

Endnotes

[1-7] *The New Dictionary of Thoughts,* p. 47.

[8] *Encyclopedia of 7700 Illustrations,* p. 190, #411.

[9] Ibid., p. 192, #419 Epigram.

[10]Chambers, Oswald. *My Upmost for His Highest* (Westwood, New Jersey: Barbour & Co., Inc. Copyright © 1987).

[11]Lea, Larry. *Could You Not Tarry One Hour?* (Altemonte Springs: Creation House, 1987).

[12]Jones. *Life Is Tremendous.*

[13]Bettger, Frank. *How I Raised Myself From Failure to Success in Selling.* (Englewood Cliffs: Prentice-Hall, 1947).

[14]Maltz, Maxwell. *Psycho-Cybernetics.* (Englewood Cliffs: New Jersey: Prentice-Hall, 1960).

[15]Cole, Edwin Louis. *Maximized Manhood* (Tulsa: Harrison House, Inc., 1985).

[16]Frankl, Viktor E. *Man's Search for Meaning.* (Boston: Beacon Press, 1962).

[17]Sumrall, Lester. *The Making of a Champion.* (Nashville: Thomas Nelson, Inc., 1987).

[18]Capps, Charles. *The Tongue — A Creative Force* (Tulsa: Harrison House, Inc., 1976).

[19]Price, Frederick K.C. *How Faith Works* (Tulsa: Harrison House, Inc., 1976).

[20]Kennedy, D. James, *Truths That Transform.* (Old Tappan: Fleming H. Revell Co., 1974).

[21]Copeland, Germaine. *Prayers That Avail Much* (Tulsa: Harrison House, Inc., 1980).

Chapter 12

RAINY DAYS AND MONDAYS

There's no education like adversity. [1]
— Benjamin Disraeli

✩✩✩✩✩✩✩✩✩✩✩✩✩✩✩✩✩✩✩✩✩✩✩✩

As soon as you decide you are going to turn your life around, pick up the pieces and go on, or set your course for a definite goal, you will have some great opportunities to quit!

Tom Landry, former coach for the Dallas Cowboys, wrote me once after the team had a difficult season:

"Van, the important thing about adversity is that it will bring out the best or the worst in all of us."

The question is not *whether* you will have adversity. You *will* have some!

And you will have "Job's comforters" to come and tell you that you cannot make it. . .that you might as well give up. . .that things will never be any different.

The Dark Night of the Soul

A day of adversity is the time when hope flees from your heart, when fear paralyzes your mind and destroys enthusiasm, when tears rush to your eyes more often than laughter.

This may be a time when you are tempted to question God's love for you, or sometimes wonder if you still believe in Him at all, or if you are really in His will.

This is the dark night of the soul, the testing hour of the spirit.

But you need to realize that adversity forces you to evaluate what you believe, what your goals are, the methods you have been using to achieve your goals. Every achiever recalls that adversity unlocked the doors to his greatest achievements.

Humility is recognizing personal limitations, being willing to accept those that cannot be changed, but also being willing to do whatever is necessary to change those that *can* be changed.

In the Gospel of Mark, there is an interesting account:

The Teacher from Galilee had been ministering. He had started early in the day, then held a "remedial learning session" for his twelve immediate followers.

Later in the day, He said to them, "Let's go over to the other side." (Mark 4:35.)

That is what this book is all about: ways to help you get "over to the other side" of wherever you are.

Getting to the Other Side

The first thing is to *decide* to cross over, to develop a vision, to get organized, to set goals and objectives, to learn to manage your time — then to be able to face adversity and win.

Look what happened as soon as the Teacher from Galilee decided to go over to the other side: He found himself in the middle of a big storm.

Perhaps you are in a storm now, possibly in your family relationships.

Perhaps it is your marriage or in your finances.

Perhaps you have problems spiritually or mentally.

Perhaps you have just had a negative report from the doctor.

I went to see a psychiatrist once about my inferiority complex.

He helped me so much.

He told me I did not have an inferiority complex — I *was* inferior!

One fellow told me his doctor gave him six months to live.

I said, "What happened?"

He said, "Oh, when I couldn't pay my bill, he gave me another six months."

Perhaps you are facing a negative report of some kind, a real storm in your life.

Perhaps you are wondering why you should face adversity, or why a storm would come to you.

☆ ☆

A storm is proof you have not yet been conquered.
A storm is opposition on the road to a miracle.
A storm always comes for a reason but only comes
*   for a season.*

☆ ☆

Often I will open the Bible to read, and a passage will say, "And it came to pass...."

I breathe a sigh of relief and say, "Thank goodness it did not come to stay!"

During a storm of adversity, if you remain teachable, then you are reachable. The good news is that you can have peace in the middle of a storm.

If you allow it, a storm will begin to wear you down, and fear will set in. Fear makes quitting seem like a viable option.

Fear stops the flow of your joy...the lack of joy saps your strength...no strength causes a loss of peace of mind...loss of peace causes your focus on your vision and goal to slip.

When you *stand* in the middle of adversity — not waver or shake or sit down and cry — you will attract attention. People will wonder what you have that enables you to stand. That does not mean you will not have some "down" days or maybe even a failure or two along the way. What it means is that you can come out on top.

State of Mind[2]

If you think you are beaten, you are.
If you think you dare not, you don't.
If you would like to win but think you can't,
It's almost a cinch that you won't.

If you think you'll lose, you have lost.
For out in the world, you will find,
Success begins with a fellow's will;
It's all in the state of mind.

For many a race is lost ere ever a step is run.
And many a coward fails ere ever his work's begun.

Think big, and your deeds will grow.
Think small, and you'll fall behind.
Think that you can, and you will.
It's all in the state of mind.

If you think you're outclassed — you are.
You have to think high to rise.
You have to be sure of yourself before
you ever can win a prize.
Life is a battle that does not always go
to the stronger or faster man.
But sooner or later, the man who wins is
the man who thinks he can.
It's all in the state of mind!

Famous trial lawyer William Jennings Bryan said:

"Never be afraid to stand with a minority that is right. For the minority that is right will one day be the majority.

"Always be afraid to stand with the majority that is wrong, for the majority that is wrong will some day be a minority."

You may be facing discouragement today, but decide to get up. Go on, and face adversity.

Many years ago, a young midwestern lawyer suffered such deep depression that his friends thought it best to keep all knives and razors away from him.

During this time, he wrote, "I am now the most miserable man living. Whether I shall ever be better, I cannot tell. I'm awfully forbode I shall not recover."

However, he was wrong. He did recover and went on to become one of America's most beloved presidents — Abraham Lincoln.

Keys to Facing Adversity

The *first* key is to face your problem realistically.

Be honest.

Be realistic.

Stop trying to assign blame.

Do not panic; do not run.

Seek qualified counsel.

☆☆☆☆☆☆☆☆☆☆☆☆☆☆☆☆☆☆☆☆☆☆☆

There are only two kinds of people to talk things over with: People who have done what you want to do and those who have paid the price you want to pay.[3]

— Charles Jones

☆☆☆☆☆☆☆☆☆☆☆☆☆☆☆☆☆☆☆☆☆☆☆

Most people are going to try to talk you out of things rather than into things.

Drop your pride, and go for help.

The *second* key is forgiveness.

If the adversity you are in was caused by someone else, decide to forgive them.

Unforgiveness will not hurt them, but it certainly will damage you!

Go to church, talk to your pastor.

Listen to uplifting cassette tapes.

Read good literature, books that motivate and stimulate.

A *third* key to coming out of the storm is to get into a new project that will give purpose to your free time and increase your energy.

Your emotions will fluctuate incredibly during storms. Allow time for events and new people to change you.

Establish new goals.

Many times, there is a tendency toward disorientation. It becomes difficult to make plans. So become decisive about some short-term accomplishments. Practice decisiveness.

A *fourth* way is to reach out to someone else going through similar problems. In helping them, you will receive healing in your own life.

When Job prayed for his friends, his own captivity was turned.

Do not disassociate from everything and become introspective.

Let your pain generate compassion for others.

Your past is fertilizer for the future. Allow the seeds of God's Word to be planted in your future. Nurture and stretch the beautiful faith that comes from knowing Him.

A *fifth* key is not to allow guilt to overwhelm you.

Guilt comes easily when you are facing problems. Avoid condemnation.

Forgive yourself as quickly as you would someone else.

Fear and anxiety are tormentors and will fragment you even more.

Be good to your mind, your body, and your emotions. If anxiety is causing depression, try to exercise and work out the tensions physically. Allow yourself to be entertained. Laughter is one of the best remedies for what ails you (whatever it is)!

A *sixth* remedy is to stay in a circle of friends who really care.

Be cautious of who you allow to come into your life during a time of adversity.

Stay near those who have proven their loyalty.

Disconnect from those who blame and accuse — evil communication corrupts and disrupts.

☆☆☆☆☆☆☆☆☆☆☆☆☆☆☆☆☆☆☆☆☆☆☆

A wise man will walk with the wise and become wiser.
A fool will walk with fools and be destroyed.

☆☆☆☆☆☆☆☆☆☆☆☆☆☆☆☆☆☆☆☆☆☆☆

When you are facing adversity is an excellent time to commit your life completely to God — which sounds simple but isn't.

As you struggle for new identity — struggle to overcome adversity and gain a new sense of worth — you have a tendency to want to pull yourself up by your own bootstraps.

God wants to be a part of your life.

Entrust your memories, as well as your ambitions, to the Lord. He wants to help you achieve your new dreams and goals. Make him Lord and Master of your future. That will guarantee total happiness and success.

How To Tell a Winner From a Loser[4]

A winner says, "Let's find out"; a loser says, "Nobody knows."

When a winner makes a mistake, he says, "I was wrong"; but when a loser makes a mistake, he says, "It wasn't my fault."

A winner goes through a problem; a loser goes around it, and never gets past it.

A winner makes commitments; a loser makes promises.

A winner says, "I'm good, but not as good as I ought to be"; and a loser says, "I'm not as bad as a lot of other people."

A winner tries to learn from those who are superior to him; a loser tries to tear down those who are superior to him.

A winner says, "There ought to be a better way to do it"; a loser says, "That's the way it's always been done here."

The ability to bounce back, to turn bad breaks into opportunities, is a trait nearly all successful people possess. Such men simply will not be defeated.

Some years ago, a buggy salesman had saved $1,000. He and a partner with half that amount planned to make rubber tires for buggies. Competitors, however, prevented them from getting a patented welding machine needed for making the tires. It seemed they were stopped even before they got started.

But the salesman would not give up. With the help of a mechanic, he devised a better and cheaper way to embed wire into the rubber.

Later, when he started to make tires for the new horseless carriages, another patent monopoly prevented his making the "clincher" type of tire. Nothing daunted, he set out to develop the "straight-side" tire.

Henry Ford liked the young man's idea and placed an order for two thousand tires.

The young man who had not given up was Harvey Firestone.

DON'T QUIT![5]

When things go wrong, as they sometimes will,
When the road you're trudging seems all uphill,
When funds are low and the debts are high,
And you want to smile, but you have to sigh,
When care is pressing you down a bit,
Rest if you must, but don't you quit.

Life is queer with its twists and turns,
As every one of us sometimes learns,
And many a failure turns about,
When he might have won had he stuck it out.
Don't give up, though the pace seems slow —
You may succeed with another blow.

Often the goal is nearer than it seems to a
        faint and faltering man.
Often the struggler has given up, when he
        might have captured the victor's cup.
And he learned too late,
        when the night slipped down,
How close he had been to the golden crown.

Success is failure turned inside out —
The silver tint of the clouds of doubt.
And you can never tell how close you are,
It may be near when it seems afar;
So stick to the fight when you're hardest hit —
It's when things seem worst that you musn't quit.

Endnotes

[1]Disraeli, Benjamin. *Dale Carnegie's Scrapbook,* p. 40.

[2]Harris, Sidney. "State of Mind."

[3]Jones, Charles. In a private conversation with the author.

[4]Harris, Sidney.

[5]"DON'T QUIT." Compliments of The A. B. Hirschfeld Press, Denver, Colorado.

Chapter 13
GO FOR IT

*The highest reward for man's toil is not
what he gets for it but what he becomes by it.*
— John Ruskin

☆☆☆☆☆☆☆☆☆☆☆☆☆☆☆☆☆☆☆☆☆☆☆☆

Madeline Manning Mims was born in the ghetto in Cleveland, Ohio. An inner city child, she was told she would never be able to get out of her environment.

Everything was against her.

But she found that she could *run* out of the ghetto when she put God on the throne of her life.

She became an Olympic Gold and Silver Medalist, qualifying for the Olympics four consecutive times over sixteen years.

In 1921 in Harlem, New York, a small boy frequently was left with relatives so his parents could go on tour with their vaudeville troupes.

His mother was mean and abusive, often venting her temper on her young son. During his childhood, he stayed with many relatives who were alcoholics. He went to eighteen different schools before he graduated from high school.

At 13, he ran away on a bicycle, heading for California hunting an aunt who lived there. When his bicycle broke down, he stole rides on freight trains, eating whatever food other hoboes left behind.

Later, he served some time in the army, then began a radio career in the late 1940s. He went on to appear on other radio shows and then television programs.

Since then, he has written two poetry anthologies, two short-story collections, several novels, and other books.

He is an accomplished musician and noted as a lyricist, having written more than four thousand songs, including scores for Broadway plays.

In addition, he is a popular lecturer, and he wrote the PBS series, "The Meeting of the Minds," a historical dramatic presentation.

But perhaps Steve Allen is best known for creating the late-night talk show format for television. The talk show he created in 1953 went on the air in 1954 as "The Tonight Show"![1]

At some time, nearly everyone must live through a storm of some kind, as we talked about in the last chapter. Perhaps it is a "broken" heart, loss of a job, breakup of a marriage. Sooner or later, adversity comes to all of us.

That is the time when we wonder if life is worth living.

We wonder, "Is the dream worth the price?"

I say, "Yes! It is."

The time when many people throw up their hands in despair, give up, and quit is the best time to *go for it*.

We look at famous people, such as Steve Allen and Madeline Mims, and say, "They made it, and I could have too *if* I had their breaks, *if* I had been in their shoes."

We think the grass is greener in our neighbors' yards.

We use our hard times as excuses to justify lack of success.

We look enviously at the successes of others, whose lives seem so glamorous.

We say, "If times weren't so tough, I could get ahead."

However, if we could take everyone's problems and put them into a big pile, then pick the ones we wanted — more than likely, we would pick our own. If we look at other people's problems, not other people's successes, our own begin to take on a new perspective.

It has been my observation over the years that 90 percent of us bring our own defeats in various ways: by too much confidence or too little, by pessimism when things look good.

This is the time to "*go for it!*"

Winners Have No Sense of Blame

The one trait common to all great and consistent winners is the absence of an attitude of blame.

They do not pout or accuse when others are at fault.

They do not rage at themselves when they are at fault.

Occasionally, they may be beaten — but they never "beat" themselves.

Over the long haul, they win more often than they lose, frequently by allowing their opponents to beat themselves.

I am convinced temperament more than talent or brains determines whether a person is self-fulfilling or self-destroying.

The difference between one champion and another may be trifling in terms of durability, but vast in terms of heart.

You hear a great deal about the "killer instinct" in champions. All that means, I believe, is that in the ultimate showdown, a champion forgets himself and concentrates with passionate intensity upon his object.

The near-champion never forgets himself, never subordinates himself to the goal or the game.

I do not believe the winning determination is really an instinct to "kill" or to "conquer," but an instinct for perfection, a determination to complete something started, a perfection so exquisite in itself that it obliterates the man achieving it.

A winner is beyond praise and beyond blame. He, or she, does not "beat" himself or fight himself, *but forgets himself.*

It is time in your life to put aside blame, to assume responsibility and accountability, but to put your eyes and your efforts on the goal.

Go for it!

Sow Good Seeds

Resist the temptation to accept a job based on convenience or pressure from friends or family. Pour yourself into something in which you can believe.

Do not panic or talk doubt. Refuse to be intimidated by people or circumstances. Be bold! Clothe courtesy with courage.

Do not mumble — look people in the eye when you speak. You are not a slave nor a "wimp."

Knowledge is power. The difference between failure and success is information.

There are two ways to learn:

• Experience (learning by your own mistakes), and

• Wisdom (learning from the mistakes of others).

Do not sell yourself short. Do not belittle yourself.

Spend time and attention on your personal growth and development. Invest in books, seminars, good clothing, and other things that will increase your confidence and sense of worth.

The better you treat yourself, the better you will be treated by others. Sow good seeds in the soil of your own life and mind.

☆☆☆☆☆☆☆☆☆☆☆☆☆☆☆☆☆☆☆☆☆☆

The force, the mass of character,
mind, heart, or soul
that a man can put into any work,
is the most important factor in that work. [2]

— A. P. Peabody

☆☆☆☆☆☆☆☆☆☆☆☆☆☆☆☆☆☆☆☆☆☆

Be quick to listen.

In the insurance industry, it is said that million-dollar producers make statements while multimillion-dollar producers ask questions.

Learn *how* to listen.

Listening is an art, an ability, and an incredible tool for personal growth.

Productive listening is vital for success.

Listening demands discipline, effort, and an unselfish attitude.

Listen to those around you, especially those who are hurting.

Listen to your own conscience, the key to real success.

Listen for the needs of others.

Listening also is "sowing good seeds."

☆ ☆

A wise man will hear and will increase in learning.
— Proverbs 1:5

Even a fool, when he holdeth his peace, is counted wise,
and he that shutteth his lips is esteemed
a man of understanding.
— Proverbs 17:28

☆ ☆

Surround Yourself With Good People

Invest time and seek the counsel of wise people. Be a student of those who succeeded before you. Appreciate the accomplishments of others.

Absorb the wisdom of others. Do not allow their personal shortcomings to dampen your enthusiasm. Take the best, and leave the rest. Value the counsel of the learned.

☆ ☆

He that walketh with wise men shall be wise.
— Proverbs 13:20

In a multitude of counselors there is safety.
— Proverbs 11:4

☆ ☆

Relationships are important to success.

The most important relationship a man ever will have is with God. Spending time with God, reading His Word, communicating with Him through prayer, and letting Him communicate with you, is the best way to be victorious.

Next in importance comes your relationship with your spouse.

Third in impact upon your life are the people you choose to surround yourself with. They can make all the difference in the world.

Paul Harvey once said to me, "Van, if you want to get big fleas, hang out with big dogs!"

You should be careful who is allowed in your inner circle of friends. I do not mean to be "stand-offish," aloof, or elitist. However, you do need to make sure that the people with whom you associate the most often are in agreement with you and encourage you to move to a higher level.

Your closest friends should be people you respect, people who are diligent and conscientious. You not only will have more fun in life, but you will reach your goals quicker.

One of the most exciting things I found in the insurance industry was the "push" I got from belonging to a study group. Most of the people in the group were more advanced in the business than I was. They had more years of experience and were doing more business.

Because of the synergistic effect of the group's coming together, sharing ideas, keeping track of each other and where everyone was in production, pulled each of us up to a level where, as individuals, we would not have reached until many years later.

✩ ✩

And the way to become truly useful is to seek the best that other brains have to offer. Use them to supplement your own, and give credit to them when they have helped.[3]
— Gordon Dean

✩ ✩

A relationship group is not meant to be a means of letting other people do your thinking for you. Far from it! Such a group is meant to stimulate your own thinking through the association with other minds.

No one person can know everything. The more sympathetic minds — by "sympathetic," I mean those working for a common purpose — the more related information is going to be available. Great ideas usually result from a combination of related information.

You can also "surround yourself" with wise people through books, tapes, and videos.

☆☆☆☆☆☆☆☆☆☆☆☆☆☆☆☆☆☆☆☆☆☆☆☆

All that mankind has done, thought, or been is lying as in magic preservation in the pages of books. [4]

— Carlyle

☆☆☆☆☆☆☆☆☆☆☆☆☆☆☆☆☆☆☆☆☆☆☆☆

Winning Attitudes

Be willing to grow into greatness.

As a small acorn grows into a great oak tree, so grow the seeds of greatness within our lives:

It takes work and discipline.

It takes proper nurturing.

It takes time and may not happen overnight.

Resist impatience. As you assume responsibility for the present, take time to enjoy the things available to you right now.

Constantly hold before you the dream toward which you work. Your mind is an incubator that gives birth to ideas and dreams.

What you concentrate on, you will feel;

What you feel, eventually, you will perform;

What you perform, you will become;

What you become determines your destiny.

What you see in your mind will happen in time — see yourself victorious, financially free, healthy, and blessed.

☆☆☆☆☆☆☆☆☆☆☆☆☆☆☆☆☆☆☆☆☆☆

Happiness is feeling good about yourself, and that depends very much on your productivity.

Productivity depends on your ability to set up a list of daily tasks in order of importance and accomplish them.

☆☆☆☆☆☆☆☆☆☆☆☆☆☆☆☆☆☆☆☆☆☆☆

Avoid a complaining attitude.

Speak with enthusiasm and authority. None of us ever gets a second chance to make a first impression. Project the impression of a winner. The way you talk, dress, and act reveals much about your character. Dress neatly. Avoid the sloppiness which suggests a careless lifestyle.

A winner never condescends but lifts others around him to a higher level of encouragement. Help others attain their success, and you will help yourself.

Go for it!

Build a climate of confidence.

Information breeds confidence. Know *what* you believe and *why* you believe it. Disconnect the memory of past failures. Stop advertising your mistakes. Remind yourself of good decisions and triumphs of the past. See yourself winning.

Deposit success pictures in the bank of your mind. Your mind is like a filing cabinet or bank vault. It stores thousands of mental photographs of what you see, hear, and think about most often.

What you think about most often is your god!

If your thoughts are constantly on money, it has become an object of worship to you. Your dominant thought patterns reveal your true values.

Manage your time.

As I said earlier, control your time, and manage it wisely. Why? Because time is money. Treat time with the wisdom it deserves. Determine what you want to accomplish each day, each week, or each month, and set deadlines for the attainment of these goals.

Avoid time wasters — bored friends, unnecessary phone calls, idle chatter.

A day that is a social success usually is a business failure.

Be merciful.

What you make happen for others, God will make happen for you.

What you sow today determines your harvest tomorrow. Sow kindness; be slow to criticize and quick to forgive. Love produces a nonjudgmental climate that will also affect you.

Become a part of someone's miracle, and it will come back to you.

Give favor and expect to receive favor. Expect others to respond favorably toward you.

Do not build mental "monsters" of fear and worry.

If a salesman expects rejection, he will multiply the possibilities and usually receive it.

Plan now for financial freedom.

Success does not "just happen." You set it in motion.

So it is with financial freedom.

You will never change where you are until you change what you are doing.

Live within your means. Do not let your upkeep be your downfall. Live with the means presently provided, and budget to correct improper and harmful spending habits.

Work hard, and be diligent, but respect your body.

Do not succumb to the "furniture disease":

That is when your chest falls into your drawers.

Health is life's first prize. Men spend their health getting wealth, then gladly pay all they have gained to get their health back!

Be good to your body. Give it sleep and proper nutrition. Exercise it, and give it the surroundings it needs. Your body is the only "machine" God will allow you during your lifetime. Value it, and take care of it.

Learn how to talk rightly, and tame your tongue.

The most powerful force in your life is your tongue. Proverbs 18:21 says, "Death and life are in the power of the tongue."

Your tongue can destroy or build, tear up or mend.

Use your words to build confidence in others. Refuse to gossip about or slander anyone else. Learn to keep confidences. To control your tongue is to control your very life.

Learn how to handle criticism.

When you decide to *go for it*, you probably will receive some.

The human heart craves acceptance and approval; rejection destroys our motivation. However, criticism can be productive or destructive, depending on how you receive it. Analyze the source, the purpose, and the solution.

Do not give any more time to a critic than you would to a friend; but, being teachable is one sign of a true winner.

Be honest.

The power of an honest life is remarkable. Integrity cannot be purchased.

There are two forces that build the gigantic machine called credibility which opens the door to success: trustworthiness and expertise.

Honesty is the hinge that swings the golden door of prosperity and success.

Never, never, never give up.

Winners are just ex-losers who got mad. The battle belongs to the persistent. The victory will go to the one who does not quit. Refuse to let friends or circumstances defeat you.

If you have been defeated, remember that from the ashes of defeat burn the greatest fires of accomplishment. Your past is the fertilizer for the future, as I said before.

God made you to climb and not crawl.

God made you to fly and not fall.

God made you to swim and not sink.

You were not made to dig in the dirt with the chickens, but to soar in the clouds with the wings of an eagle.

Go for it!

Today is *your* day.

Endnotes

[1]DeMaris, Ovid. "The Other Side of Laughter; the Pain the Gain, the Life of Steve Allen," *Parade Magazine,* pp. 4-9. Reprinted with permission from *Parade,* Copyright © May 5, 1985.

[2]*The New Dictionary,* p. 741.

[3]Quote from the late Gordon Dean, former chairman of the Atomic Energy Commission. Taken from *Sourcebook of 500 Illustrations* by Robert G. Lee, p. 100. Copyright © 1964 by Zondervan Publishing House. Used by permission.

[4]Tan. *Encyclopedia of Illustrations,* p. 215, #550.

Conclusion:

THE POWER
CONNECTION

Now unto him that is able to do exceeding abundantly above all that we ask or think, according to the power that worketh in us.

— Ephesians 3:20

I am thankful for the exposure to success motivation principles and concepts in how to develop a positive mental attitude. It *is* possible to use success motivation techniques, and a positive mental attitude can help us look and be successful by the world's standards.

However, it is impossible to get a genuine new direction, new life, or to fight to "stay in the game" without a relationship with God through His Son, Jesus Christ.

What a turning point came when I invited Christ into my life. Christianity is the only religion in which the One being worshiped comes to live in us. God did not send Jesus simply to get us out of hell and into heaven. God sent Jesus to get God out of heaven and into us!

What a dynamic difference when as believers we become God-inside minded. When we receive a revelation of the Creator living in us, we know:

> *We can have what the Bible says we can have!*
> *We can do what the Bible says we can do!*
> *We can be what the Bible says we can be!*

As a believer, I began to understand the integrity of God's Word, *God is not a man that he should lie; neither the son of man, that he should repent: hath he said and shall he not do it? or hath he spoken, and shall he not make it good?* (Num. 23:19). God meant what He said and said what He meant! He indeed does watch over his word to perform it (Jer. 1:12). He desires to show himself strong in your life (2 Chron. 16:9).

The other Bible truth that began to transform me was the reality of the redemption, what Jesus bought and paid for when He died for you and me at Calvary. My need was to receive, to relax in the facts. When Jesus said, *It is finished*, healing, preservation, deliverance, and soundness became mine when I believe it is by faith.

Until 1978 by most standards, I might have been considered a success. A beautiful wife, two wonderful children, Wendy and Brent, a growing insurance practice with membership in the prestigious Million Dollar Roundtable. As I began to pursue a closer walk with God, the storm clouds began to roll in. A troubled marriage soon produced trouble with the children, the business, and the walls came tumbling down. Not only did I want to quit, I practically did!

In 1979 I found myself living with Vince Evans who was the quarterback for the Chicago Bears football team. God used this experience to teach us both and to open the door for me to serve as chaplain for the Bears under the covering of the Fellowship of Christian Athletes.

God also began to open the door to ministry with the nation's major league baseball teams through Baseball Chapel, Inc. In the past, I have had the privilege to serve both the Chicago Cubs and White Sox as chapel coordinator. At the same time, doors to America's corporations and trade associations began to open with speaking opportunities all across the country.

The point is simply this — *decide to stay in the game*! God seems to delight in taking man's mess and working a miracle. It can happen for you. You can get started today!

To experience a real change in your family, finances, career, or whatever, you must find out what the Bible says about that particular area. Then you can make a decision upon which you can base your life. God's Word is His will. When continuing to grow in Christ seemed like only a dream, I began to see that, like many Christians, I was not appropriating what already was mine through the death, burial, and resurrection of Jesus. I needed to read and understand the last will and testament of Jesus so I could begin to enjoy my inheritance.

The problem: I was not walking by faith, and Hebrews 11:6 says that without faith, it is not possible to please God.

You and I are built for a divine connection. We are constructed from creation to "plug in" to God, and He to you — your mind demands negotiation, and your heart seeks companionship. Each human being has a "God-sized hole" in his or her heart that can only be filled by Jesus.

No amount of seeking to satisfy that hunger, that emptiness, through relationships with other people, through a career, money, and possessions, or through adventure and entertainment will work.

Something draws each person toward God, although he may never have heard the Gospel.

You were created for accomplishment.

You were engineered for success.

You were endowed with the seeds of greatness.

You are God's number-one interest.

Calvary revealed the intensity of His love. If something is good for you, and you are His child, He will place it within your reach. (Ps. 84:11.)

Faith demands an object before it can be released.

Evaluate your spiritual gifts and abilities, if you already are a Christian, and then decide to *go for it*. Pursue the career for which God equipped you. If you are not a child of God, please keep reading.

How To Become a Child of God

That if thou shalt confess with thy mouth the Lord Jesus, and shalt believe in thine heart that God hath raised Him from the dead, thou shalt be saved.

For with the heart man believeth unto righteousness; and with the mouth confession is made unto salvation.
— Romans 10:9,10

For God so loved the world, that He gave His only begotten Son, that whosoever believeth in Him should not perish, but have everlasting life.

For God sent not his Son into the world to condemn the world; but that the world through Him might be saved.

He that believeth on Him is not condemned; but he that believeth not is condemned already, because he hath not believed in the name of the only begotten Son of God.
— John 3:16-18

Those five verses contain the proof and the way of salvation.

Accept Jesus in your heart:

"Jesus, come into my heart and cleanse me from all unrighteousness. I accept you as my Savior, Healer, Deliverer, and Lord. Change my life to conform to your image."

Then, my friend, I guarantee you will not only stay in the game, but you will spend eternity with the King of Kings and the Lord of Lords.

Your desire to grow in Christ by reading this book is the mark of a leader, and I appreciate your example.

In the Introduction, I made you a promise. If this book has helped you turn your life around, I would like to hear from you.

I personally pray that you will find true happiness and success in God, and I desire that your life will show an improved quality of living from reading the concepts and thoughts that have helped me and many others like me.

ABOUT THE AUTHOR

Van Crouch is founder and president of the consulting firm Van Crouch Communications, dedicated to challenging individuals to achieve excellence in their lives.

As a consultant to business professionals, as well as sports professionals — including baseball, NBA basketball, football, and hockey players — Van inspires a winning attitude.

His experience with pro teams, including the Super Bowl champion, the Chicago Bears, and in the corporate world gives him an enthusiasm for life and a vision for victory.

After ranking as a top ten sales leader with American Express, Van went on to receive many outstanding awards for his work in the insurance industry. During his years in insurance, he became a qualifying member of the Million Dollar Round Table.

In demand as a speaker all over the country, Van addresses sales meetings, conventions, banquets, seminars, trade associations, and appears frequently on various nationwide radio and television programs.

He is an active speaker for numerous NFL teams and for Baseball Chapel. Also, he is sports director for WCFC-TV in Chicago.

In addition, he speaks to many Christian organizations and ministries, as well as churches, schools, and universities.

He and his wife, Doni, live in Wheaton, Illinois.

Other Products Available from Honor Books

Laughing Your Way to Excellence Video
by Van Crouch

Van inspires a winning attitude. *Laughing Your Way to Excellence* is a message of honesty and no compromise with good clean humor that will challenge you to live for God in today's world.

Let one of America's leading humorists and public speakers help you find new direction and motivation to achieve excellence.

VVC-001/$19.95 ISBN 1-56292-003-3

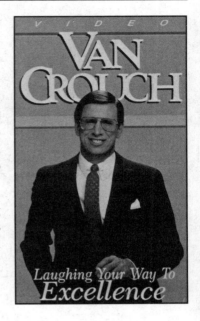

Laughing Your Way to Excellence Audio Cassettes
by Van Crouch

This dynamic message recorded at the Century Plaza Hotel in Los Angeles, California, is filled with hard-hitting humor that will have you laughing. Van's quick wit and insight will inspire you to face life with new enthusiasm.

TVC-001/$15.00

"Van Crouch relates Christian principles to contemporary problems with clarity and conviction. Splendid speaker!"
—Paul Harvey
PAUL HARVEY NEWS
AMERICAN BROADCASTING CO.

tempus.™ *Timesaver Christian Personal Organizer System*

Save your time and money and quit putting it off — get organized! **tempus.**™ **Timesaver** creates more time for you. Be more effective at work, at home and in your Christian walk. Using your

tempus.™ **Timesaver** guarantees you more time for God, love, family, career, plus physical and mental fitness! Show those you love that you care.

WARNING: Using **tempus.**™ ***Timesaver** has led to an increase in efficiency at home, in the office, and in prayer times. Consistent use results in a loss of disorganization and a gain of personal productivity and confidence.*

tempus.™ **System 365** — *2-pages-for-each-day format* TEM-365/$69.95
tempus.™ **System 52** — *2 pages-for-each-week format* TEM-52/$59.95

Dare To Succeed

The perfect gift for inspiring success in life!

- Scripture promises for success in life and career
- Inspiring and motivating quotes from great leaders
- A special word by author/teacher Og Mandino
- Scriptural prayers for life and career
- Guidelines on finances, goal setting and time management
- A 31-Day devotional and a Read-Through-the-Bible program
- A great birthday gift, or any special occasion

Bound in burgundy bonded leather.
HB-001/$19.95 ISBN 1-56292-001-4

Van Crouch is widely regarded as one of the best and more versatile speakers in America. As the founder and President of the consulting firm, Van Crouch Communications, Van challenges individuals to achieve excellence in their lives. Van's experiences in the corporate arena and as a speaker to many of the nation's professional sports teams, give him an enthusiasm for life, a spontaneous sense of humor, and a genuine interest in people.

After ranking as a consistent sales leader with the American Express Company, Van went on to receive many awards for outstanding performance in the insurance industry and has been a qualifying member of the Million Dollar Roundtable. Crouch has authored the best selling book *Stay In The Game* and is a frequent guest on numerous radio

"Here's hoping, Van, the day will come when we are able to do some work together. You do a marvelous job. God bless you and your activities."
—**Zig Ziglar**

"We were most fortunate to have acquired the services of a person such as yourself. You have played an expanded role toward duration of our winning tradition. Thank you for your efforts."
Tom Landry
Former Head Coach
Dallas Cowboys

and television programs.

Van is in demand for his thought-provoking seminars and keynote engagements to Fortune 500 companies, government organizations, church groups and management and sales conventions worldwide.

Van Crouch has the ability to motivate people to raise their level of expectation. he will cause your attitude to become more positive, your problems smaller, your self-esteem and confidence will grow and yolur self-doubts disintegrate. He is sure to both inspire and challenge you.

VAN'S SPEECHES COVER A WIDE RANGE OF TOPICS

"Destined To Win."

A powerful message that will affect your thoughts and actions long after Van's final sentences have shaken your composure.

"On The Growing Edge."

Leadership is a growing process. An inspiring message of the possibilities, goals, necessity and methods of this growing process needed to develop true leadership potential.

"Developing Competitive Excellence."

A stimulating address designed to help you discover the amazing person you truly are.

HIS SEMINARS ARE DIRECT AND TO-THE-POINT

"Get It Done Now!"

This seminar guarantees you the power to achieve far more in far less time. Learn how to set and achieve goals, how to manage your time and how to make personal and corporate organizational plans.

"The Hour of Sales Power."

A sales clinic designed with the professional sales person in mind. Special emphasis on closing and persuasive technology.

"Grow Toward Leadership."

To grow in executive leadership it is necessary to study human nature. A highly informative seminar concerning the essentials of good human relationships, and team building. For middle and top management.

"In the age of self manufactured credentials, it's refreshing to hear someone focus on the development of character. From the locker room to the boardroom, no one delivers a more powerful message with integrity and credibility. Being part of a Van Crouch seminar can change your life forever... and it's really fun."

**Arnold "Nick" Carter
V. P. Communications
Nightingale-Conant
Corporation**

"The coaches, players and staff of the Chicago Bears truly appreciate your interest, leadership and time spent in furthering and interpreting the "Good News."

"It is our wish that you will continue to help and inspire our players in the coming year. Thank you again for a job well done."

**Mike Ditka
Head Football Coach
Chicago Bears, NFL
Champions Super Bowl XX**

"Van Crouch is one of the few people who bats 1000 all the time. Your sincerity and knowledge of sales, coupled with your professional platform ability, makes you a very unique speaker. I knew you were going to be good, but you far surpassed what we were expecting."

**Charles Jones
President/ CEO
Life Management
Services, Inc.**

"I was always thankful that Van Crouch wasn't an NFL linebacker, because he's the hardest-hitting speaker I've ever heard!"

**Walter Payton
Chicago Bears, NFL
(Retired)
Champions Super
Bowl XX**

For information about Van Crouch's seminars,
speaking engagements, cassette tapes and videos,
write:

Van Crouch
1137 Wheaton Oaks Drive
Wheaton, Illinois 60187

Additional copies
of *Stay in the Game*
are available from your local bookstore
or by writing:

P. O. Box 55388
Tulsa, Oklahoma 74155